The Kick Ass College Guide to Presentations

CREATE AWESOME PRESENTATIONS, SPEAK LIKE A PRO, RULE THE WORLD

By Brian Stampfl

Published by Duthie Hill Press, LLC
ISBN-13: 978-1544944135
ISBN-10:1544944136

D1367673

CONTENTS

A Note to My Readers 1
Death and Public Speaking - An Introduction to Both 3

Section 1: Kick Ass Journey to Awesome

CHAPTER 1: Becoming Bulletproof 9
CHAPTER 2: Overcoming Fear 12
    Fear is a Clue We Need to Prepare Better 14
CHAPTER 3: Entertaining a Room Full of Lawyers 18
CHAPTER 4: Studying the Greats - Develop Your Style 22
    Discovering Your Own Inspiration 28

Section 2: Kick Ass Preparation Techniques

CHAPTER 5: Where Do I Start? 33
    Critical Question #1: How Much Time Do You
    Have For Your Presentation? 34
    Critical Question #2: What's Your Method of Delivery? 34
    Critical Question #3: What's Your Topic? 39
CHAPTER 6: Brainstorming 101 41

Section 3: Kick Ass Technical Stuff

CHAPTER 7: Technically Speaking 47
    Presentation Software 49
    Back It All Up 51
CHAPTER 8: The PowerPoint Build Begins 53
    PowerPoint Help 54
CHAPTER 9: The Rule of Three 56
    The Three Types of Learners 58
    The Three Types of Delivery 60
CHAPTER 10: How to Create Kick Ass Content 63
    Start with an Explosion 63
CHAPTER 11: How Many Slides Should I Create? 69
    Just Tell Me How Many Slides I Need! 72
    How Long is This Build Going to Take? 74

CHAPTER 12: Building the Framework _ _ _ _ _ _ _ _ _ _ _ _ _76
  The Layout _78
CHAPTER 13: Text _80
  Font Choice _82
  Font Color _82
  Font Size _83
  Spelling and Grammar _ _ _ _ _ _ _ _ _ _ _ _ _ _ _ _ _ _ _84
CHAPTER 14: Photograph File Size and Resolution _ _ _ _ _ _86
  Picture Quality _86
  Screen Brightness _87
  Highlighting Details on a Picture _ _ _ _ _ _ _ _ _ _ _ _ _ _88
CHAPTER 15: Video _90
CHAPTER 16: Transitions and Animations _ _ _ _ _ _ _ _ _ _93
CHAPTER 17: Object Alignment _ _ _ _ _ _ _ _ _ _ _ _ _ _ _96
  Visually Balanced _97
CHAPTER 18: Relevancy _ _ _ _ _ _ _ _ _ _ _ _ _ _ _ _ _ _ _99

Section 4: Kick Ass List of Extras

CHAPTER 19: Props _103
CHAPTER 20: All the Gadgets _ _ _ _ _ _ _ _ _ _ _ _ _ _ _ _108
  Remote Control or Keyboard? _ _ _ _ _ _ _ _ _ _ _ _ _ _ _108
  Microphones and Podiums _ _ _ _ _ _ _ _ _ _ _ _ _ _ _ _ _109
  Laser Pointers _111
  Where's Technical Support? _ _ _ _ _ _ _ _ _ _ _ _ _ _ _ _112
CHAPTER 21: Room Configuration _ _ _ _ _ _ _ _ _ _ _ _ _114
  Lights On or Off? _115
  Handouts _116

Section 5: Kick Ass Way to Move and Talk

CHAPTER 22: What Comes Out of Your Mouth _ _ _ _ _ _ _121
  Command Presence _121
  Know Your Stuff - But Don't Memorize Your Stuff _ _ _ _ _123
CHAPTER 23: The Screen Is Not Your Audience _ _ _ _ _ _ _126
  Never Read to the Audience _ _ _ _ _ _ _ _ _ _ _ _ _ _ _ _127
  Ah, Um, and You Know _ _ _ _ _ _ _ _ _ _ _ _ _ _ _ _ _ _128
CHAPTER 24: Practice for Time _ _ _ _ _ _ _ _ _ _ _ _ _ _ _130
CHAPTER 25: Humor _132
CHAPTER 26: Body Talk _ _ _ _ _ _ _ _ _ _ _ _ _ _ _ _ _ _ _135
  Why We Do What We Do - A Primal Response _ _ _ _ _ _ _135
  The Distance to Here _ _ _ _ _ _ _ _ _ _ _ _ _ _ _ _ _ _ _136

Building Barriers_____137
What Do I Do With My Hands?_____137
Focus on Your Eyes_____139
Control Your Body_____141
CHAPTER 27: What Not to Wear_____144

Section 6: Kick Ass Art of Audience Engagement

CHAPTER 28: The Art of Audience Engagement_____151
The Three Types of Crowds_____151
Taming a Wild Audience_____156
CHAPTER 29: Crash and Burn - When Things Go Wrong____163
What the Crowd Don't Know, the Crowd Don't Know___163
When You've Forgotten Everything You Know_____164
Tongue-Tied_____165
Proof That Recovery is Possible_____166

Section 7: Kick Ass Show Time

CHAPTER 30: Showtime_____171
Last Minute Checklist_____172

About the Author_____173

A Note to My Readers

This book is the result of over fifteen years of speaking experience compressed into a guidebook designed for maximum efficiency. Everything between these pages is based on my experiences as a public speaker, a presenter, a trainer, a student, and as a former adjunct university instructor. I've not only given my fair share of presentations, I've tortured my own students by requiring them to present as well. As a life-long student of public speaking, I've had the opportunity to study the best, and sit through the worst, learning a few things along the way.

What I offer are straightforward instructions on how to develop your assigned topic, or create one if you don't yet have one. You'll learn how to build a PowerPoint[1] presentation that will convey your message to your audience without sending them into a coma. You'll get tips on how you can look like a professional presenter while avoiding the most common pitfalls suffered by amateurs. I've included a few stories of both personal success and failure that have given me the experience necessary to write this book. And if you're willing to follow my guidelines, you'll have the tools necessary to create a solid presentation that will likely earn you maximum credit for whatever assignment you've been given.

Lastly, this book is a direct reflection of my teaching style and who I am as a person. I'm all about getting the job done, being direct, and calling things as I see them. My hope is that you're thick-skinned enough to not be offended by my direct approach and skewed sense of humor. As the title of this book, "The Kick Ass College Guide to Presentations" implies, this is not your average book on speeches and presentations. This is a book for those who believe that good enough is what everyone else is doing. What you're looking for is excellence and this book delivers it!

---

[1] PowerPoint is a registered trademark of Microsoft Corporation.

Death and Public Speaking
An Introduction to Both

Search the Internet for "greatest fears," and you'll find surveys that frequently rank public speaking as the number one all-time greatest fear. Death on the other hand comes in around fourth or fifth on the fear scale, with fear of flying and spiders taking second and third. I can understand the spider thing, but what motivates people who think public speaking is a fate literally worse than death?

If you trust these surveys, that means there are people running around who'd rather die than give a speech. This strikes me as a bit of an overreaction. I know I've certainly suffered a few butterflies in my stomach while presenting, but I've never stood on stage hoping a firing squad would rise from the audience and put me out of my misery. We speak in front of other people all the time. But why is it that by simply moving to the front of the classroom or onto a stage we go from what should be a normal activity to the equivalent of a nightmare?

Despite public speaking's odd ranking on the fear scale, I acknowledge that standing in front of a group of people to speak can be scary, or at least unnerving. We practice the art of talking with each other every day of our lives, but when we have the full attention of everyone in the room and an expectation of performance, the game changes.

Unfortunately for most of us, it wasn't until some high school teacher or college professor required us to give a classroom presentation that we were forced to actually think about how to do one. Suddenly, with little to no advanced training on how to create a presentation, we were required to figure out what we were doing on our own. Add the pressure of possible embarrassment in front of our classmates and a fight for a decent grade, it's no wonder that people are terrified of public speaking. We've been thrown head first into a task we know little to nothing about and are expected to perform. This is not a learning model that I would recommend to anyone.

The good news is that by reading this book you'll be able to quickly learn the skills necessary to deliver a high quality presentation, without the element of fear. We'll start at the ground level and address the issues that make public speaking a scary proposition. You may be surprised to learn what I believe to be the actual cause of fear when it comes to public speaking and how easy it is to eliminate it. We'll discuss topic development. This will include a brainstorming exercise that requires you to hang your head over the side of a couch, followed by ways to create your own speaking style.

There's also a ton of information on building the ultimate PowerPoint presentation that will not only provide you with your own *safety net* to ensure your success, but will capture your audience's attention. By the way, I'll be using the term *PowerPoint presentation* throughout this book, but will discuss a variety of media options in the *Presentation Software* section coming up.

Later, we'll cover everything you need to know about how to move your body on stage, how to speak like a pro, and even how to interact with the audience. And if that's not enough, there are multiple tips and tricks on how to recover in the event you find yourself struggling during your presentation. Presentation success is quite simple once you know all the tricks, and they're all here!

I've discovered through my own experience there are two key factors that support any successful presentation. If everything you do during your preparation strengthens one of these two factors, you're on your way to success. Your presentation will not only be something that your audience will be impressed with, but you'll ensure that you've delivered the content necessary to get the best grade possible. So what are these amazing factors that will turn you into a grade "A" presentation machine?

➤Kick Ass Key Factor #1: Know Your Stuff

Of all the topics I will be covering, this is the theme that will show up in some form or the other with great frequency. Why? Because if you know your topic inside and out, you can eliminate fear. And in the world of public speaking, fear comes from believing that failure is not only possible, it's probable. The unprepared speaker is obsessed they will forget mid-flight what it is they're supposed to be saying. I'll show you how to prepare for your presentation, whether it's fifteen minutes or two hours long, so that you'll have an actual grasp of the materials you're presenting. You'll not only know what it is you should say, you'll actually know what you're talking about. Armed with the confidence that you know your topic inside and out, your speech will be as fluid as normal conversation.

➤Kick Ass Key Factor #2: Build Your Presentation So You Can't Forget Your Stuff

What if I told you there's a way to format your PowerPoint presentation so that it is virtually impossible to get stuck or forget what it is you are planning to say? Think of it. Your PowerPoint will not only serve as visual reinforcement to your newfound impressive delivery style, it will double as your personal roadmap. Using the advice in this book, you'll create an amazing PowerPoint layout that will take you from start to finish, while ensuring you don't get lost along the way. Add that to the vast amount of other practical advice, all based on my personal experience, and you'll be able to overcome the most common obstacles faced by presenters. This includes forgetting your own name mid-sentence, going too fast or too slow, dealing with difficult audience members, taking questions, and a host of other "oh no, kill me now" moments that would make mere mortals crumble from the stress. In short, the guidelines in this book will not only turn you into an amazing presenter, you'll have the confidence to know that you are darn near bulletproof. And dare I say, you just might enjoy the process!

Lastly, I suspect that a few of you may already have some presentation experience. Your goal may be to simply pick up a few tips rather than go for the full-meal-deal. If that's your situation, you'll find that this book is comprised of small chunks of information. Check the *Table of Contents* for the topic of your choice and you can focus on just what you need to know. For the rest of you, start at the beginning and read all the way through. This book is packed with information, blended with my personal speaking experiences and observations that will put everything you'll learn into perspective.

This is it. This is your survival guide. These are the skills and tricks used by the best speakers in the industry, and there's no reason why you can't use them for yourself.

Now, let's go build a presentation that's Kick Ass!

Section 1

Kick Ass Journey to Awesome

CHAPTER 1
Becoming Bulletproof

"LUCK is not a factor. HOPE is not a strategy. FEAR is not an option."
~ JAMES CAMERON

Imagine walking into your classroom, head held up high, knowing that today's your day. You don't give a rip whether you go first or last. Heck, you could postpone it until tomorrow. Makes no difference to you. You're not that student who just wants to *get it over with.* You know your stuff, your presentation is solid, you've got your PowerPoint on three different back-ups, and there's not a question about your topic you can't answer. It's all second nature. Your teacher ought to give you an "A" grade now, just to save time.

It may not seem like it now, but what I just described is not a fantasy, but very doable. There's no reason why you can't be so comfortably prepared with your presentation that breathing is more of a challenge than having to stand in front of your class and talk. While I'd stop short of saying that it's easy to create a great presentation, I know that even without this book, doing a little extra work will put you ahead of the average student. And that's not some put-down of the average student, it's a reality that I've personally observed and been a part of. *When it comes to presentations, many students do just enough to get by.* It's also possible that up until now, you may've been one of those students. However, by following even a few of my recommendations found throughout this book, I can assure you that you'll likely be in the top 90% of presenters in your entire school. Outrageous claim you say? Not really. As I said in the introduction, public speaking ranks at the top of our greatest fears. It's not like the average student is spending a tremendous amount of time practicing what scares them to death. Public speaking and presentations aren't hard, they're just not something most people want to work at.

And while average is good for most, performing at the 90th percentile is usually considered very good for others. But what about that last 10%? Who's filling the space between 90 and 100? I'll tell you. The top 10% is where the pros go, and the good news is that you can go there, too. Is there even better news?

The difference between a good presentation and an awesome one is a small amount of extra work, attention to detail, and a willingness to take a chance.

I'm going to ask you to at least consider the possibility of taking your presentation skills one step higher than you previously imagined. I'm talking about separating yourself from the crowd and moving from an average presenter to one of the best. I hope that you'll want greatness, because it is attainable. And once you've become comfortable with public speaking, you might find that it's fun to have the undivided attention of a group of people who are interested in what you have to say.

In the first section of this book, I'll give you some tips on how to overcome the public speaker's greatest obstacle: Fear. Next, I'll introduce you to four modern speakers who, in my opinion, have mastered the art of delivery in their unique field. Their linked videos demonstrate everything that I talk about in this book. If you want to experience excellence before you begin creating your own, let these amazing people become your mentors. Finally, I'll direct you to the world's greatest video catalog of speakers where you'll be able to study the styles of the best in the business. You'll have access to hundreds of videos demonstrating that presentations, done right, can in fact become a craft.

Set your goals, choose your mentors, and be prepared to be excellent.

CHAPTER 2
Overcoming Fear

The sound of your own heartbeat can be deafening. Sweaty palms are usually followed by the butterflies in your stomach. You search for the exits, think of excuses why you should not have to present, and even consider faking a medical emergency. But now, positioned at the podium, you look out into the crowd and see that all eyes are upon you. You can shuffle your notes, straighten your clothes, scratch an itch, and pray for a natural disaster, but no amount of wishful thinking is going to change your situation. You have a presentation to do, and now it's showtime!

As the first word rolls off your tongue, you pray that you're actually speaking in the correct language. By the second word, your inner dialogue tells you that one mistake will be the beginning of an avalanche of life altering embarrassment for everyone to see. The audience will be watching your final act on earth. It will be as if you were diving, head first...into a toilet.

The horrors of public speaking are different for all people. But I suspect that the previously described symptoms are not too far off for many. But why is public speaking so scary? Coupled with my own experiences and an informal survey of those who actually rank public speaking as being scarier than death, I've identified some basic generalizations of things that scare us when we set foot in front of a live audience.

1. Participation is Not an Option
You are mandated to speak. When you're having a conversation with several people, there is a give and take

process that allows each person to say their part and then stop. The next person picks up where you left off, they say their piece, and the process continues. In a group discussion, you can say as much as your friends will tolerate or you can sit quietly and listen. No stress. However, the option to sit quietly and take it all in doesn't exist while defending your thesis to an audience. Public speaking requires you to speak for a set period of time. It's amazing how scary speaking to others can become when we're required to do it.

2. Screwing Up is Equal to Death

I once had an instructor point out that embarrassment was an emotion reserved only for humans. He used the example of a horse running through a field. If the horse tripped and fell, the horse would not get up, flushed in the face, and die of embarrassment. He'd just keep on running. And the other horses certainly wouldn't point and laugh at him. Being concerned that you might make an error (Gasp!) should not be a fear, it should be an expectation. Mistakes will be made, but it's how you respond to them that counts. Don't worry, we'll cover what to do when things go wrong later in the book.

3. Forgetting Your Own Name

Having experienced this firsthand, I can equate this to driving from one location to another and having no memory of the actual trip. It's as if you wake up from a dream, only to find yourself standing on stage and not knowing what you're supposed to be talking about. *Brain farts* are common, but building safety nets into your presentation will help you recover in the event you fall.

4. Stinking at Presentations

Believing that we are not good at a particular thing is a great excuse for not trying. For example, I believe very strongly that I stink at playing golf. Strangely enough, I don't actually play golf. It's a self-fulfilling prophecy and an argument I can't lose. Apply the same circular logic to presentations: I stink at presentations - I don't do presentations - See, I told you that I stink at presentations. I've actually had conversations that sounded like this. Fortunately, there is a solution!

5. Generally Unidentifiable Fear
Since there is no way for me to cover all the reasons people fear public speaking or the symptoms that result, I'll make a generalized assumption that you may just not wish to do it. You may not even blame fear as one of your reasons. The preparation, the process, and the hassle is enough to deter you from even taking the first step. I get it, it's not for everybody. But despite your internal battle, you've got a job to do. Sometimes the best way to start is to take the first step, then the second, and repeat as necessary. In the words of Nike, "Just Do It."

➤Fear is a Clue We Need to Prepare Better

As I've said earlier, the simple solution to all your fears comes from adequate preparation and knowing the material you're presenting very well. The second trick is to create a safety net that will give you the cues necessary to keep you from forgetting your stuff and make it possible to quickly recover if you run into trouble. But beyond preparation and safety nets, there are some fundamental facts that you should know to help you alleviate your fears, whatever they may be.

We're All Friends Here
Classrooms are filled with students. Unless you sit in class each day with a paper bag over your head, you've likely gotten to know some of these people. In fact, I'd go so far as to say that some of them might be your friends. You're able to sit around in groups, answer the teacher's questions and

experience no fear of speaking in public. When you talk with your classmates or engage in dialogue with your teacher, you are actually *Speaking in Public*. This is important to think about as you approach the podium or front of the classroom. Yes, all eyes are upon you and you have the floor. But remember, these are the same people you were interacting with prior to giving your presentation. Here's more great news:

- Your classmates are your friends.
- Everyone wants you to succeed.
- Nobody cares if you make a mistake.
- They are worried about their own presentations, not you.

Yeah, But I Don't Know These People

Oddly enough, you can have conversations with strangers, too. If time permits, I'll often walk around and introduce myself to as many audience members as I can, prior to speaking. Getting to know some of the audience ahead of time is a great way for me to relax and get rid of my nervousness.

Being familiar with your audience and having that connection will give you a surprising boost of confidence. As I said, confidence is fear's greatest enemy and you'll want to be armed with as much as possible. The side benefit to connecting with your audience is how you will make *them* feel, as well. Most people will feel honored that you've introduced yourself and made an effort to learn their name. Do this and you'll have all kinds of support from an audience that's pulling for you to succeed. We'll talk in more detail later about making a connection with your audience. But for now, if you don't have a few friends in the audience, make some. And even if that's not possible, I have some more good news:

- Strangers in the audience are one handshake from being your friend.
- The audience wants you to succeed.
- They don't care if you make a mistake.
- Any audience wants to learn, be entertained, and be supportive.

But I'm Worried What People Will Think

Why? Who cares what people think? I realize that dismissing what people think is not as easy as it sounds. Having people say or think badly of us is a fear in and of itself. For that reason, we often approach those things that scare us by not taking chances and playing it safe. Safe means that we won't be criticized and therefore we've avoided fear. Notice I said *avoided,* and not *beaten* fear.

Truth be told, I care what people think, generally. But I put what people think into two categories. The first are those who are critical just for the sake of being critical. We all have those kind of people in our lives. These are the ones who complain about everything, and often for no apparent reason. Give them one hundred dollars and they'll complain that it's not two hundred. I may hear what a person like this has to say, but I probably won't be too concerned with their message.

On the other hand, I do care when someone gives me honest feedback about my performance. That doesn't mean that I have to agree with them, but if someone genuinely cares about you and wants you to succeed, then this might be someone whose opinion is worth considering. And keep in mind if two or more people offer feedback suggesting an area for improvement, it's really worth considering. For example, if two people from the audience suggest that you need to speak louder so the back row can hear you, seriously consider this feedback. A recommendation from two people, such as "speak louder," is such an insignificant request that it has credibility. This is usable information and beats a negative comment from a naysayer such as, "Your presentation stinks and so do you."   Not exactly actionable criticism, is it?

A New Way of Thinking
As we continue on, I'm going to ask you to step way outside of your comfort zone. I'll also ask you to consider the idea that in order to be awesome, you'll need to create not only a presentation but be prepared to give a *performance.*

Before I explain what giving a performance actually means, in the next chapter I'll share a story in which I learned firsthand the power of a "performance" over a run-of the-mill presentation.

CHAPTER 3
Entertaining a Room Full of Lawyers

Once, I received a phone call from a colleague asking if I wanted to present at an upcoming conference for a group of attorneys. I wasn't given much information other than they needed professionals who could speak about law-related topics. I reluctantly agreed.

As the conference date approached, I called my contact to clarify what information I should cover in my presentation. She didn't know or care, and told me to call the conference organizers and ask them. When I did, I got an answer something like, "Well, just speak about whatever you normally speak about." I wasn't thrilled with this response. Granted, since my background was in crime scene investigation, this was obviously the topic that I should cover. But I didn't have any guidelines as to what they needed to know within the ninety minutes I was allotted. I'd have to figure something out on my own.

As the date approached, I became more and more irritated about having committed to the conference and felt as if I was being used to simply fill a time slot. I was angry that my time was being wasted, and I promised myself to never accept a request to speak at a conference ever again.

On the day of the event, as I was driving to the Washington State Convention Center, my negative self-talk had gotten to the point that not only had I sworn-off ever doing a speaking gig again, I decided that I would go out in style. My plan was to take this event and make it my own. Instead of acting all serious for a bunch of stuffy attorneys, I was going to tell jokes, use funny voices, flap my arms, and turn the event into an act of pure self-entertainment. I knew that I'd never see these people again, and I certainly had no plans to return.

When I walked into the auditorium, I was surprised to see that there were about 150 people seated and ready to go. I wasn't nervous and I didn't care. I looked around at each person's face as if to challenge them to enjoy what was about to be my final presentation.

A woman from the conference walked up to the podium and introduced me as the next speaker. She butchered the pronunciation of my last name, as I've grown accustomed to. Before speaking, I unhooked the microphone from the podium stand and walked off the stage. I stood down on the floor level, in front of the crowd. Not only do I do funny voices, I have some great facial expressions and I wanted to be sure my audience could see them.

And then I began...

Just to see their reactions, I started off talking slowly and in a monotone voice. I did this for about twenty-seconds as I introduced my topic. I almost started laughing as the faces in the audience turned from a look of moderate interest to the realization that this may be the longest hour and a half of their lives. Before anyone stood up to leave, I changed the pace just to see what would happen. I started talking really fast as I told them my background. The expressions changed to a look of confusion.

Then I turned to my PowerPoint presentation. And although I planned on being less than professional, my PowerPoint was recycled from several previous presentations and contained some of my best material. As I continued on, I tried to incorporate as many jokes as came to mind. I wanted to see if I could loosen up these stuffed shirts, or at least irritate them a bit. I used funny voices while telling my stories, and allowed myself to be as animated as I could without getting myself thrown out. And then a strange thing happened.

The audience started laughing at my jokes, and some even began smiling. They were doing exactly what one might expect when hearing someone tell jokes, but I was still annoyed that I even had to be there. At this point, I was conflicted. Then it got even stranger. Several people from the audience started raising their hands to ask questions. Not only did it look like they were having fun, these people wanted to learn more. This was not the expected outcome, but I took their questions and answered them the best I could. Despite my half-hearted attempt at self-sabotage, I had inadvertently formed a connection with the audience. As a result, the ninety minutes rapidly flew by and I was done.

When I left, I was exhausted, but it felt great to be done. I'd met my obligation to the conference, delivered the appropriate information to the attendees, and entertained myself in my farewell-to-all-future-presentations tour. I was out of there, never to return again!

Several weeks later, I got a call from one of the conference organizers. He asked for my email address and wanted to know if I wanted copies of the evaluations filled out by the attendees who heard me speak. I told him I didn't think I could handle being criticized by that many people at one time. He replied that I may have actually been the most popular speaker at the conference. I almost dropped the phone!

When the evaluations arrived, I was dumbfounded. What I

thought was supposed to be my ticket to never being asked to speak again turned into something else. The evaluations contained some amazing comments: "Excellent speaker," "Be sure to invite him back next year," "Very informative," "Best speaker at the conference," etc., etc.

It was this event that forever changed the way I looked at public speaking and presenting to a crowd. Although I'd been comfortable speaking prior to this event, I had never received compliments such as this before. And it was from this event I learned the secret to making a good presentation great. I learned that I needed to loosen up, lighten up, and not care what anyone thought.

It was on this day that I discovered that the best presentations are actually...performances!

CHAPTER 4
Studying the Greats - Develop Your Style

If you want to blow your competition out of the water, or just be an amazing public speaker and presenter, the best advice I can give you is to study the people who rock at their craft. This is the same advice that someone would need if they wanted to improve in any type of sport or specialized skill. Get out there, watch the pros, and figure out what they're doing right. When you see something that grabs your attention, figure out a way to take that *thing* with you.

But how, you ask?

Each time I've attended any type of event, whether it included speakers, presenters, or any type of training, I've paid attention. I've kept a notebook handy and written down those things that I thought really worked well to keep my attention and helped to deliver the point. I also kept note of all the nonsense speakers committed that either irritated me or caused the audience to run for the exits. In fact, it's years of prolific note-taking while sitting through some of the best and worst presentations that made this book possible.

But wait, what is that I hear you saying?

"I don't have the time, nor the interest, to sit through years of presentations to find some little nugget of who-knows-what just to bring my presentation skills up one notch."

Who said you had to?

Get Ready For the Fast Track!

Allow me to direct you to some of the world's greatest speakers and presenters. And you don't even have to leave the comfort of your computer to see them. Below, I have examples of people who've not only been an inspiration in my life, but are absolute rock stars when it comes to delivering their message.

I've provided the URL to each of the names of the speaking pros below to a video of what they do best. If you prefer, search the person's name and the title of their talk for a faster result. There is a short explanation as to why I've chosen that particular person, and I've given you a heads-up as to what you should be watching for so you might be able to incorporate it into your presentation style.

By the way, everything I think makes these people great is detailed later in this book. Whether it's movement, speaking style, use of props or whatever, I've got it covered.

Anthony (Tony) Robbins - Motivational Speaker, Entrepreneur and Author

Tony Robbins may be the most successful self-help guru in the world. With over 25 years of experience speaking to audience-filled auditoriums for several days at a time, he delivers powerful messages that drive people to action.

This video, entitled "How to Influence People and Get What You Want" (www.youtube.com/watch?v=FoRBZ1pZs-Q) is a segment of one of Tony's multi-day conferences. The topic he covers in this segment is about rapport building. It's about 23 minutes long, but Tony's ability to project his message will be apparent within the first few.

Points to Watch For:

What I find inspirational about Tony's speaking style is exactly what you should be looking for in his video: Command Presence. Granted, he's six foot, seven inches tall, and has a deep, gravelly voice. But even if he were a little dude, I think that he'd still be able to get people's attention. That's because command presence comes out not only when you know your material extremely well, but also when you speak with confidence and authority. It's one of the essential differences between experts and amateurs.

Here are some other things to watch for:

- Inflection in Voice
- Emphasis of Key Words
- Passion of Delivery
- Subject Matter Expertise
- Free Flow of Hands

Robin Williams (1951 - 2014) - Comedian and Actor

Robin Williams was pure genius. And it's through Robin's stand-up comedy I prove my idea that the best presentations are actually performances. Think about it. Is stand-up comedy so different from doing a presentation? I'd argue that the goal is the same. Deliver a message in a way that your audience is receptive to what you have to say. And Robin Williams was masterful in his ability to deliver multiple messages in a way the audience loved.

Before we go on, keep in mind that I'm not suggesting you turn your presentation into a stand-up comedy routine. That might be fun, but not likely what your Social Studies professor is expecting. However, I do believe in making presentations fun and memorable.

This video from 1982 is entitled, "Robin Williams as the American Flag" (www.youtube.com/watch?v=Q_L1vLv84vs). At five minutes long, Robin's performance is packed with take-aways that you can easily incorporate into your presentation. Since this video is actually quite entertaining, I'd recommend watching the video for fun the first time through just to see why he remains my favorite comedian and performer of all time. Then watch it again, but this time search for the points I've listed below.

Points to Watch For:

Notice first off that Robin is basing his routine on what may seem like a narrow topic, *The American Flag*. An overwhelmed student might receive this as a topic from their instructor and struggle to come up with material worthy of a 20 minute presentation. But here you'll see that there are all kinds of subtopics surrounding the flag. Among other things, Robin talks about the creator of the flag, the stars and the states they represent, the meaning of the various ways the flag is flown, and the symbolism of the flag.

Here are some other things to watch for:

- Use of Props
- Use of Hands
- Body Movement
- Use of Stage
- Passion of Delivery

Amanda "Fucking" Palmer - Musician "The Dresden Dolls", Author and TED[1] Speaker

I learned about Amanda via my favorite podcast, "The Tim Ferriss Show" (fourhourworkweek.com/podcast/). The podcast is titled, "Amanda Palmer on How to Fight, Meditate, and Make Good Art." (fourhourworkweek.com/2015/03/30/amanda-palmer/). I'd never heard of her before, but during the interview she spoke in great detail about her process for developing her TED talk, "The Art of Asking," (www.ted.com/talks/amanda_palmer_the_art_of_asking) which is just under fourteen minutes long. The discussion about her creative process is reason enough to listen to this interview. I was fascinated to learn about how much heart and effort she put into preparing what appears to be an effortless presentation. Even as a veteran performer and musician, Amanda suffered the same challenges as any college student having to stand before an audience and deliver their best.

Of the four recommendations in this section, "The Art of Asking" is my favorite. However, if you opt to listen to the podcast interview with Tim Ferriss, a word of warning: The interview is filled with colorful language that may be offensive to some listeners. But if you want to hear a fantastic interview with an inspirational artist, including Amanda's funny explanation about how she acquired her stage name, you're gonna have to take a listen.

Points to Watch For:

The first few moments of this presentation demonstrate the power of silence. Notice that the preparation and presentation of the props create an uneasy, perhaps even haunting sort of feeling for the audience. When Amanda finally speaks, the monotone quality of her voice helps to maintain that tension until she reveals her first PowerPoint slide. You can feel the tension subside as the audience releases their breath. These are subtle techniques, but quite powerful for injecting emotion into a presentation.

Here are some other things to watch for:

- Use of Props
- Storytelling
- Emotional Connection
- Passion of Delivery

Steve Jobs (1955 - 2011) - Co-founder of Apple Computer

If you're at all familiar with Steve Jobs' speaking and presentation style, there are two sources you may be drawing from. The MacWorld computer shows in which Steve's keynote speeches, later dubbed "Stevenotes," have been regarded as events in and of themselves. Granted, his purpose at these events was to debut the newest products from Apple, including the iPod, iPad, iPhone, and the newest Apple computers. But his strength was his ability to connect with the audience while debuting the latest gadget from Apple. And it was from these presentations Steve became famous for the catch phrase, "One more thing." This signature line was his cue to the audience that the last thing he was going to talk about was going to be the biggest.

Since there are so many MacWorld keynotes to draw from, I'd recommend a search using the keywords, *Steve Jobs MacWorld*, and then include your favorite Apple device, as it was likely debuted by Steve himself. I'm partial to his introduction of the iPhone at MacWorld 2007 (https:// youtu.be/9hUIxyE2Ns8). And if you decide you want to learn more about Jobs' techniques and preparation for his keynotes, consider reading the book, *"The Presentation Secrets of Steve Jobs"* by Carmine Gallo. You'll learn much of what I cover in this book, but you'll get deeper into the weeds of planning and developing your presentation.

The other source you may be familiar with is Steve's 2005 Stanford Commencement Address (www.youtube.com/

watch?v=UF8uR6Z6KLc). Of the links I've provided, this one demonstrates how to tackle a more traditional speech. There is no PowerPoint, Steve is fixed at a podium, and he uses notes for reference. Regardless of whatever you're preparing for, I highly recommend this video for one technique he's very good at, and that's good storytelling.

Here are some other things to watch for:

- Powerful Message
- Delivery Style
- Emotional Connection
- Proper Use of Notes
- Eye Contact

Keep in mind, these are people who I've drawn inspiration from to develop my own presentation style. There are many reasons to like what these great speakers have to offer. However, you may want to develop a presentation style that's completely left of center, and unlike what every college student has been doing for the last thirty years. In fact, I encourage you to do just that! Find your own source of inspiration and grab up tips and tricks that fit your personality. Find speakers whose topics are of your own interest. Branch out even further and study your favorite performers in all the arts you enjoy. Take everything you discover and use it to develop your own unique performance style.

►Discovering Your Own Inspiration

Your absolute best resource for finding videos of amazing presentations and speakers is at TED.com. The acronym TED stands for Technology, Entertainment and Design and the topics discussed loosely fall into one of those three categories. Taken from their website, "TED is a nonprofit devoted to spreading ideas, usually in the form of short, powerful talks (18 minutes or less)." I'll add that there's a handful of presentations that are just three to four minutes long. These videos are great examples of how you can pack a lot of information into a very short period of time.

The beauty of TED is that because all the presentations are eighteen minutes or less, you can see exactly what it takes to do a presentation that is similar in length to yours. You can search for your topic of interest using key words or draw from the category menus. Regardless of the topic you choose to watch, know that the speaker is an invited guest to the TED conference and is not being paid to speak. Speaking at a TED conference, regardless of who you are, is considered to be a privilege (although I hear the speakers get a great SWAG bag for their effort). Because of the prestige that comes with being a guest speaker at a TED conference, the speakers know they have to bring their "A" game.

To get you started, here are some more recommendations:

Adam Savage - The man from MythBusters! He's one of my favorites for taking topics that, on the surface, seem as if they would be difficult to expand on and turning them into a fascinating eighteen minutes. Check out these two videos:

"My Love Letter to Cosplay" (www.ted.com/talks/adam_savage_my_love_letter_to_cosplay?utm_source=tedcomshare&utm_medium=referral&utm_campaign=tedspread)

"My Obsession With Objects and the Stories They Tell" (www.ted.com/talks/adam_savage_s_obsessions?utm_source=tedcomshare&utm_medium=referral&utm_camp

aign=tedspread)

Brene Brown - I know her as an author. But with over twenty-six million views on TED, she is a TED favorite. Check out:

"The Power of Vulnerability" (www.ted.com/talks/ b r e n e _ b r o w n _ o n _ v u l n e r a b i l i t y ? utm_source=tedcomshare&utm_medium=referral&utm_camp aign=tedspread)

Jill Bolte Taylor - A brain scientist has the opportunity to study her own brain as she suffers a stroke. Give her extra credit for introducing one of the coolest props ever. This is a scientist's approach to presenting. Check out:

"My Stroke of Insight" (www.ted.com/talks/ jill_bolte_taylor_s_powerful_stroke_of_insight? utm_source=tedcomshare&utm_medium=referral&utm_camp aign=tedspread)

[1] Technology, Entertainment and Design

Section 2

Kick Ass Preparation Techniques

CHAPTER 5
Where Do I Start?

A common side-effect of most any difficult project is *decision paralysis*. Spending hours thinking about the title of your presentation or what color font you're going to use (in lieu of actually getting started) are symptoms of this condition. Luckily, the cure is to not worry about the heavy details right now, but begin moving forward. And if you don't know where to start, don't worry, I've got you covered. Follow these steps and the details will fall into place.

I'll assume that since you're reading this book that you've been given some sort of an assignment and need a little guidance on how to either develop or refine your topic. That means you likely have some clue as to what your presentation is going to be about. That's a good place to start.

On second thought, it's entirely possible you really are suffering from decision paralysis because your instructor is "allowing" you to research and choose your speaking topic. Hopefully, you've been given better direction than to pick a topic within the subject of say, *World History*. When the guidelines for choosing a topic become too broad, the decision becomes harder. Having too many choices leads to decision-making overload and followed by the aforementioned paralysis. Wouldn't it be much easier if your instructor insisted your topic choices were either *Option A* or *Option B*? Often, that is not the case, however.

In order to get things moving, you're going to have to first establish the parameters for your presentation. That's a fancy way of saying that you'll have to determine some basic information that will become the framework for everything else you build. This can be done by answering three Critical Questions:

1) How Much Time Are You Given For Your Presentation?

2) What is Your Method of Delivery?

3) What is Your Topic?

Pay attention to the order of the Critical Questions. The answer to the first question will help you determine your *delivery method*, and from there, the *delivery method* may shape the decision about your *topic*.

To find the answers to these Critical Questions, you're going to have to roll up your sleeves for the first round of hard work.

➤Critical Question #1: How Much Time Do You Have For Your Presentation?

This may require little or no thinking on your part, unless your instructor forgot to mention how much time you'll have. But rest assured, you're not going to be given endless amounts of time to speak, even if you want it. Know the answer to this Critical Question and it will become clear that you'll need to build your presentation to fit within that timeframe.

Later, we'll discuss how to customize the amount of information to fit your timeframe.

➤Critical Question #2: What's Your Method of Delivery?

Once you know how much time you'll have to speak, you'll want to determine what you should be doing during that time. Hopefully, you'll have some control as to the format and delivery method of your presentation. Your instructor, or even the venue in which you're speaking, will sometimes dictate how you'll have to present to your audience. For example, if you're required to speak in a public park during a sunny day, you most likely won't be able to use a projector and PowerPoint presentation. On the other hand, your science class professor may insist on you standing at the front of the class, armed only with note-filled flashcards. But no matter what method you choose (or is forced upon you), it's your job to take that delivery method and make it as awesome as you can.

No matter what delivery method you choose, there will be tips and tricks throughout this book that you can incorporate into your presentation. And as you're making your decision, keep in mind that your job is to not only deliver your message to your audience, but to do it in such a way so they actually enjoy hearing what it is you have to say.

Reading From Flash Cards - If you were forced to do book report presentations in the 5th grade, this is likely the technique you had to use. But don't worry, this is not a technique exclusive to 5th graders. The occasional Keynote Speaker at a large event has been known to use it as well! Flashcards work well as a means to organize your thoughts in a logical order and remind yourself of each point you want to make about your topic.

The drawback to Flash Cards is that you must be able to glance down at a bullet point list consisting of short phrases or words as a means to prompt your memory and keep your speech moving. Knowing your material well is something that I will continue to insist on throughout this book. If you do in fact know your material, Flash Cards can be a good tool.

Beware of the *I waited until the last moment to prepare my speech* Flash Card trap. This lazy approach often turns from what should be short and concise bullet points on a 3" x 5" card, into long drawn out text, filling the entire card surface. The unfortunate result is that come speech time, your face will be buried into your cards, desperately trying to read your compressed handwriting. Bullet points, if you managed to even create any, tend to identify the beginning of entire paragraphs. This draws the speaker into the trap of reading those same paragraphs in their entirety to the audience. Now, why is that a problem? See below:

Reading From Your Paper - This disastrous technique is more painful than someone reading a vacuum cleaner manual as a bedtime story. Unless it's a poetry reading, and I mean good poetry, reading your presentation will sound monotone and lack the voice inflections employed by a polished professional. This translates to *boring*! Even if you're a great writer, text often lacks the flow of normal speech, making the words that roll out sound dull and uninspiring. Reading to a group of people is much different from simply talking to them. You will lack eye contact with your audience, the ability to move around, and audience connection. Bottom line, it will sound terrible.

But wait, my teacher is making us do this.

On the far chance your teacher has instructed your class to each read their presentations from a sheet of paper verbatim, then your teacher is a cruel person and will die alone. Luckily, if you've been forced into this situation, there's still hope.

If you've ever been to a book reading or other event in which the author reads an excerpt from their book, then you'll know that it's possible to read something verbatim and have it still sound interesting. My best advice is to make the writing sound as much like normal speech as possible. You can test the quality of your writing by reading your paper out loud, first to yourself and then to anyone who'll listen. Change any words or even sentences that don't sound like normal speech, or more specifically, *your* normal speech.

For example, when speaking, most people use contractions when possible, because it flows better. So instead of writing *it is* or *I am*, you should write *it's* or *I'm*. This change alone will make your writing easier to listen to. The same thing applies to language that might sound okay when written, but sounds kind of strange when spoken aloud. For example:

Written Word: *The family exited the building.*
Spoken Word: *The family left the building.*

Written Word: *The plastic beverage receptacle was deposited on the counter.*
Spoken Word: *The cup was set on the counter.*

These may be subtle changes, but it's the difference between sounding like a normal person and having the audience think you're reading the ingredients of a shampoo bottle.

Your choice of individual words can also have an impact on how you sound. Unless the terminology you're using fits within the topic you're speaking about, avoid using ten-dollar words when normal speech will work just fine. Trying to sound intelligent by using fancy words that don't fit the context of your presentation, or are not likely to be understood by your audience, puts people off. I personally cringe whenever I hear someone use the word *matrix* or *vanguard* in any setting, let alone in a presentation. I'm not suggesting that you should dumb yourself down for your presentation. I'm suggesting that you speak in a manner that is consistent with normal conversation and appropriate for your audience.

Memorization - Memorizing your speech or presentation is not an easy task, and it can be difficult to recall while standing in front of an audience. In fact, I'm going to recommend against memorization altogether. Even a short presentation can be challenging without some kind of notes or other cues to keep you on track. However, if you're obligated to use this method, it's really much better to memorize only the points you want to make and not an entire script. These would be the same points you might list on flash cards, if you were using those. With just the points memorized, you can approach your speech as if you were telling a story in your own words rather than hoping that you'll remember every word. By taking the storytelling approach, you'll sound more natural and less like you're reading from your paper.

PowerPoint - Undoubtedly this may be the best presentation option available since it addresses the learning styles of most people. But poorly constructed PowerPoint presentations have been known to bring grown men to tears, cause spontaneous human combustion, and may in fact be linked to premature balding. The term *Death by PowerPoint* is real and if you've had to sit through one of these jam-packed festivals of stupidity, then you understand what I mean. For that reason, a large part of this book addresses how to create an amazing PowerPoint (or whatever software you prefer) presentation.

Group Presentation – If your instructor is making you give a group presentation, it's because he's cruel and wants to watch you struggle through the process. I'm sorry, there's no other explanation for this torturous practice and here's why:

Inevitably, five people will be assigned to work together and create a presentation. One of those five will be a stoner and will be of little value. Another will be a very nice person, but he or she will have missed several classes and will have no idea what's going on. The third person will be dealing with some life crisis and will not be able to attend the after-class planning meetings. This person will only be able to email their portion of the presentation to someone else in the group. This leaves two moderately competent students to do all the work. Ironically though, all five will show up on the day of the presentation, and each will receive full credit.

If you're assigned to do a group presentation, keep in mind that everything in this book still applies. Your group will at least need to start with the three Critical Questions in order to create the framework. The biggest challenge with group presentations is getting everyone to commit to doing their fair share of the work. If you yourself are committed to the project, it might be a good idea to have each member of the group read the portions of this book that are applicable to them. At a minimum, your PowerPoint builders should read the section on building PowerPoints, and everyone who will be presenting should read the section on delivery.

►Critical Question #3: What's Your Topic?

There are a million topics in this world. Luckily, you'll only need one. If you've been able to answer the first two Critical Questions, you should have an idea as to how long your presentation will be and your method of delivery. The last part of the three-part equation is to decide what your topic will be. Unfortunately, this may be the hardest part.

While I have no way of knowing what the subject is you'll want to present, I do have some ideas on how to make a decision. Now, clear your mind, I'm going to teach you about Brainstorming.

CHAPTER 6
Brainstorming 101

The first step in coming up with a great idea is to take the stress out of the process. Some of the world's most successful tech companies have rooms dedicated just for brainstorming product ideas. They are filled with beanbag chairs, pool tables, ping pong tables, X-Boxes, toys, latte machines, snack foods, and other fun comfort items. I've seen pictures in which some of the most tech-savvy engineers in the world were flopped sideways on colorful couches, turned upside-down on beanbag chairs, and laid out on the floor while discussing their next big product idea. It's a complete reversal from the traditional idea that anything good must be difficult, and therefore shouldn't be fun.

The reason for a playful environment is to allow these brainiacs to enter into a childlike state and allow their imaginations to run wild. You can do the same by simply placing yourself in an environment that is comfortable and free of distractions. If sitting in your favorite chair or hanging your head over the end of a couch does the job, so be it. You might even find that your favorite coffee shop, a park, or any environment that sparks creativity or inspiration will work as well. If you're going to work with others on your idea, make sure that everyone agrees that this is meant to be serious but fun. While crazy ideas may spark laughter, everyone must be free to express themselves without embarrassment or the risk of being teased. This is not the exercise you want to take on when you don't feel free to express your ideas for fear someone may give you grief in return.

When it comes time to start the brainstorming process,

have a seat in your comfy chair or relax in whatever environment takes you to your happy place. Now follow these steps:

- Have pen and paper or white board at the ready. Someone is going to need to do some writing.

- Whether alone or in a group, agree that there are no dumb ideas. If an idea pops into your head, write it down.

- As quickly as you or your assistant can write, bark out ideas related to the general subject you're asked to speak about.

- Use abbreviations if possible. If your general topic is American Presidents and President Abraham Lincoln pops into your head, just write *Lincoln.*

- Write ideas down for at least ten minutes straight. Write everything you know about your particular topic. Go fast and plan on filling your paper.

- At the end of ten minutes, or when you feel you've done a complete brain dump, pick out five topics that most closely fit what you need to speak about.

Fine Tuning - Even if you don't like the five topics that you've chosen, don't worry, you're not going to use them. I'll explain this point soon. Now is the time to split the topic down into smaller chunks. Unless you plan on teaching a full university course entitled American History, your presentation is likely slated to be somewhere between five and fifteen minutes. If you're doing a presentation at a seminar, training course, or even defending your thesis, then you will likely be presenting for somewhere between 20 to 90 minutes. Regardless of how long you have, you'll be much better off if you reduce the topic down to a manageable size.

Let's return to our general topic of American Presidents. You're not likely going to have enough time to talk about *all* of the American Presidents, and nobody wants to hear about all of them in one afternoon, anyway. Following the four steps below, we can go from a very broad topic down to a narrow segment within that same topic.

Start With — *American Presidents* — too broad a topic

Next, Pick a President — *Abraham Lincoln* — better, but he served four years

An Event Within His Presidency — *The assassination of Abraham Lincoln* — still too long

Even Narrower — *The events leading up to his death* — manageable size

Regardless of the amount of time you have to present, you'll likely find that narrowing down your topic will make it feel less daunting, and in many cases, more interesting. Take our example above. Everyone in your history class will know that John Wilkes Booth shot Lincoln while he sat in the presidential booth of Ford's Theatre. I would argue that in order to fully discuss that event, you would likely need more time than you've been allotted. The other problem is that any topic that is common knowledge presents the risk of being uninteresting. Would you rather hear a speech about something you were familiar with or be enlightened with new information?

Continuing with our example, when has anyone created a presentation focussed on what the Ford Theatre looked like, the panic that set in after Lincoln was shot, or discussed how it was even possible for Booth to get near the president? By narrowing your topic, you may find it easier to conduct your research since you'll know precisely what it is you need to know. Take your original broad topic ideas and look for the less obvious, more narrow segments within that topic. By doing so, you'll discover topics that are more manageable, and perhaps those that have rarely been explored.

Here are some more examples of how to reduce a large topic down into a more manageable one:

Broad Topic	**Narrowed Down**	**Even More Narrow**
Cinema	Movies of the 70's	Horror Movies of the 70's
American Auto Industry	Ford Motor Company	Ford Muscle Cars
Forensic Science	DNA to Solve Crimes	How to Collect DNA
Major US Companies	Big Box Retailers	Walmart™
Dogs of the World	Dogs Used for Work	Types of Police Dogs
Amusement Parks	Roller Coasters	Wooden Roller Coasters

Time, Delivery and Topic. Once you've answered these three Critical Questions, you'll find that this information is the foundation of your presentation. Now, it's time to build!

Section 3

Kick Ass Technical Stuff

CHAPTER 7
Technically Speaking

"To Err is Human. To Really Screw Things Up Requires a Computer."
~ Anonymous

Our success is often dictated by those things we can control. But what happens when you're presented with technical problems you never knew needed controlling? Since we're about to venture into the creation (or *build* as I like to call it) of our PowerPoint presentation, there are a few technical matters you should consider beforehand. As I've learned the hard way, these are not minor considerations and not something to explore moments before your turn to speak.

Here's a partial list of things to consider:

- What kind of computer will you use? PC or Mac?

- Will you build on a PC and then present on a Mac? Or vice versa?

- Will you build your presentation on one computer then run it on another?

- If transferring to another computer, what storage device will you use?

- Will your storage device work on the computer you intend to use?

- Will a projector be provided or will you need to provide one?

- Do you have the proper cables?

- Will the cables provided fit your computer?

- Does your presentation have sound?

- Will speakers be made available to you, or will you have to provide your own?

This was an easy list of questions to create, primarily because I've personally had to think through each of these problems ahead of time or improvise when the problems presented themselves. I've literally shown up at locations where I was told that a projector would be available, only to find the cables didn't fit my computer. I once had a presentation filled with videos only to find that while there were audio speakers available in the auditorium, there was no method for connecting them to a computer. And while I used to burn all my presentations to a DVD-R, I've discovered that disk drives are not available on many newer computers.

All of these small technical details are generally easy to address, but well worth troubleshooting ahead of time.

Failure to troubleshoot ahead of time could definitely derail your ability to display your PowerPoint presentation, requiring you to either postpone your presentation, or worse yet, wing it.

Preparation is one of the keys to success and you don't need some easily preventable technical glitch knocking you out of the game. I'll cover a few strategic approaches to the technical stuff, but it will serve you well to think tactically before it's too late!

➤Presentation Software

Throughout this book, I will be referring to your multimedia creation as your PowerPoint presentation. While there are several presentation softwares available, the odds are high you'll be using Microsoft PowerPoint. But no matter which application you choose, my formatting recommendations and suggested content are universally applicable. Regardless of your software's special features, at no time will I be telling you to use fonts that are shaped like teddy bears or use Star Wars-themed transition sound effects. We're going pro, and doing so looks the same regardless of the software you use. And if you still haven't decided on software, this is a short rundown of the most common options.

PowerPoint for the PC - this is definitely the most common presentation software available. If you own a PC or are going to use a computer supplied by your school or the organization hosting the event, expect this software most of the time. In fact, if you're looking for a straightforward recommendation from me, go with PowerPoint for the PC. Sticking to the most commonly used software will reduce your chances of compatibility problems caused by transferring across platforms (e.g., Mac to PC). It'll also give you a bigger catalog of *Help* options (books, videos, and online) if you need assistance, and you'll have a larger group of friends who can assist you if you need it.

PowerPoint for the Mac – if you have a Macintosh Computer, PowerPoint is available as part of the Office for Mac software package. This version of PowerPoint looks a bit different from its PC counterpart, but its function is similar. One advantage of the Mac version is that it has a much nicer collection of backgrounds and style options, making this version feel newer and more up to date than the PC version. But regardless of whether you create your presentation on the Mac or PC side, your final product should work on both platforms. I have successfully built numerous presentations on my Mac, then run the presentation on a PC and vice versa. Keep in mind that regardless of the computer (Mac or PC), the PowerPoint software from each is simply reading the file you've created.

Compatibility shouldn't be a problem. However, while I have complete trust that transferring files between platforms will work, why risk it? I recommend that you test your final product on the computer you plan to use for your presentation ahead of time. This is especially true if you're using videos, sounds, or unique fonts. Compatibility testing should never take place in front of your audience!

Keynote – this is Apple's presentation software. According to Apple, Keynote works on both the Mac and PC platforms and you can even import PowerPoint files into Keynote and edit them as needed. To some degree, Keynote is an easier and more intuitive program to use because it doesn't have as many tools and options as PowerPoint. I like this since the options that are missing are those I would never recommend using, anyway. The benefit of fewer options is a potentially cleaner looking presentation. That's not to say, however, you can't make a mess of your presentation using Keynote. You just don't have as many ways to do so. Another cool feature of Keynote is that Apple has made it possible to store your Keynote presentations in iCloud. This will allow you to run your presentation from any computer as long as you have internet access.

Prezi.com – There are a number of online presentation sites, and Prezi.com is a popular example of one. While I've not personally used Prezi, I've seen some beautiful presentations created using this site. But keep in mind that any software you use online will come at a cost. Even if it says that it's free, you may be obligated to permanently store your presentation online, allowing access to anyone who wants it. Some sites may subject you to advertising (hopefully not inserted into your presentation), but in most cases, you'll have to pay a fee of some sort. Beware of subscriptions or other tactics in which the company's website continues to charge a monthly fee well beyond your need for their service. Lastly, be aware of how your presentation will actually be displayed. These sites may require you to download software in order to run the presentation. If you're able to run your presentation from the site itself, you will likely need access to the internet.

➤Back It All Up

Creating a backup of your PowerPoint project may be the cheapest insurance you'll ever come across. A simple copy stored somewhere other than on the computer that holds the original, is your best bet. And I suggest that you make copies of your work as you progress, not just the final product. I know from personal experience and observation that files can become corrupt, work can be misplaced, and in some cases, the file just plain disappears from the computer. Throw in the potential for computer theft, fire, flood, or sabotage, and suddenly that little bit of extra work doesn't seem like such a bad idea.

In addition to backing up the master copy on your computer, you'll want to have an extra copy on hand at the time of your presentation. If you're using a thumb drive to transport your presentation to class, burn a copy to a second thumb drive. If the first copy or the thumb drive itself fails, you can pull out the second thumb drive and you'll be ready to go.

Important Note: Whenever you transfer a PowerPoint presentation from your computer to some other medium, such as a thumb drive or CD/DVD, you must put your presentation through the same rigorous function testing as your master file. This will ensure that videos, transitions, sounds, or the basic functions are working properly. If your presentation is going to become corrupt in some manner, it's most likely to occur when you make a transfer.

CHAPTER 8
The PowerPoint Build Begins

Before we can begin our PowerPoint journey together, I have an important announcement to make. It's the secret that every presenter who chooses to use PowerPoint in their presentation must know. Understand this basic concept and you can avoid the most common pitfall known to man, or at least to those who've ever had to do a presentation. This simple secret is the basis for my minimalistic approach to building a quality PowerPoint presentation that will help you deliver your message and make you look like a pro.

Your PowerPoint is Not the Presentation!

Think of PowerPoint as merely a supplement to your presentation. It is a subtle enhancement to the greatest part of your performance, and that's you. The belief that each slide projected onto the screen should be filled with tons of text, bullet points, and special effects is misguided. PowerPoint is a feature-rich program that allows for excessive amounts of information and creativity to explode onto the screen. Unfortunately, this power has lured many people into believing that the more crap they can cram into a slide, the better the product. The reality is that huge amounts of text tumbling onto the screen, lame animations, and sound effects are distractors. Those distractors draw attention toward the screen and away from you. The audience becomes torn between seeing what's projected and listening to what you have to say. The result for your audience varies between overload and boredom.

And just one more reminder:

You'll never improve a poorly thought-out presentation by projecting garbage onto the screen.

Let's begin...

➤PowerPoint Help

Just a heads up: this is not "PowerPoint for Dummies." I won't be providing specific instructions on how to use PowerPoint or any other presentation software. PowerPoint is a massive program with frequently updated versions spread out over two platforms. My goal is not to teach you how to use PowerPoint, but rather give you guidance on what content you should include and how to properly display it.

If you need specific help with PowerPoint or some other presentation software, Google.com is your friend. I've found the answer to every question I've ever had about PowerPoint by searching the web. Many of my search results have included links to videos that showed me exactly what I needed to know. I've found that the best search results came from posing my exact question to include the search term *PowerPoint*. An example would be: *How do I align multiple images in PowerPoint?* This is the best method for learning how to use this complex program quickly. You may also consider going directly to YouTube.com, since many instructional videos will be available there.

If you prefer an old school learning style, drop the search term *PowerPoint* into Amazon.com and you'll find tons of books and quick-reference guides on the topic. Lastly, PowerPoint has its own *Help* menu built into the program.

Unfortunately, I've found it to be useful only about 20% of the time. This is because you're directed to a specific function. It does not give guidance for tasks that may have multiple steps. When the internal *Help* menu fails to give me what I need, it's back to Google for me.

CHAPTER 9
The Rule of Three

Before you begin creating a presentation in PowerPoint, I highly recommend drafting an outline of your presentation beforehand. And while I don't care much for rules, I recommend a formatting process called *The Rule of Three*.

The Rule of Three simply directs us to expand each segment of the outline into three parts. For example, say you have three main sections of your presentation: a beginning, a middle, and an end. Within each of those sections are three categories of support, and within the categories of support are three supporting details. The three supporting details may then have an additional three supporting details, and on it goes. The benefit of using *The Rule of Three* is that it creates a natural flow in your delivery and prevents you from loading up your slides with endless bulleted lists. It also encourages you to expand your content where it may be lacking and condense those areas that need to be reeled in.

The following is an example of how *The Rule of Three* could be applied to a presentation in which you want to compel the audience to take your viewpoint regarding a specific topic:

Beginning

Introduction - Yourself and the Topic
My Name
Short Bio
Topic Name

Preview - Tell Audience What to Expect
Describe the Problem
Explain Popular Opinions
Why to Think My Way

Historical Background - Ensures Everyone Knows the Backstory
In 1945, a Thing Occurred
Company "X" Responded This Way
Today, the Problem is This

Middle

Description of What is Happening in the World
This Thing is Occurring
This is the Result
Long-Term Ramifications

Explanation of the Common Opinions on the Topic
Party "Y" Thinks This Way
Party "Z" Thinks Another Way
Party "A" Has No Idea

My Viewpoint and Why it's Correct
This is What I Think
This is Why I'm Right
This is the Benefit of My Thinking

End

Call to Action - What the Audience Should Do or Think
This is What I Want From You
This is Who You Should Tell
This is Your Benefit

Recap of My Viewpoint and the Benefit

This is What I Think
This is Why I'm Right
This is the Benefit of My Thinking

Request for Questions

This is a simple outline that would work well for any type of speech in which you are trying to compel your audience to think a certain way. It could be your position on a political topic, what type of soap to use, why dogs are better than cats, or who should be elected president. But keep in mind that *The Rule of Three* is a format used to create outlines, which then becomes the basis for your PowerPoint presentation. Your verbiage will vary depending on your topic. For example, if your topic is a comparison of real estate markets in two locations, you'll still have a *beginning*, *middle* and *end*. Just tweak the categories of support and then the supporting details to fit your needs.

Lastly, I want to make sure you understand *The Rule of Three* is a guideline. While balancing your outline into segments of three is an elegant approach, if you find that you have four categories of support or must introduce five supporting details, well that's what you have to do. Don't feel forced to throw out information if it's critical to your topic. Simply use *The Rule of Three* as a starting point and balance your outline the best you can without sacrificing meaningful content.

➤The Three Types of Learners

When you're trying to decide what you want to include in your PowerPoint presentation, it's a good idea to consider the various ways in which people learn. In general, most people are identified as either being an *Auditory*, *Visual*, or *Hands-On* learner. You'll likely be able to identify your dominant learning method, but the reality is that we learn through a combination of all three. For that reason, incorporating as many of the three learning styles into your presentation as possible will benefit a greater number of people in your audience.

Auditory

I trust that since you'll be giving a presentation, you'll actually be speaking to your audience at some point. It's those words you'll speak that will capture the attention of your *Auditory* learners. Yes, all of the learning types will hear your voice and hopefully listen to what you have to say. But the *Auditory* learner will pay extra attention, since hearing the information will be their dominant learning style. Keep in mind that in addition to your speaking, you could include video in your presentation with a spoken narrative. Music or sound clips, if used properly, can be added to make your presentation that much more interesting.

Visual

This is the biggest benefit of a multimedia presentation. Outside of the presenter, nothing speaks to an audience like imagery projected onto a screen. Careful selection of your photographs, videos, graphs, logos, background, and even your font style and color can capture the attention of your audience. There is so much potential for you to convey information to not just the *Visual* learners, but to everyone in attendance. This is where you'll have to give careful consideration to what information you want each slide to convey. I'll be covering more on how to layout your slides and offer some content recommendations. But you'll be making the final decision about how you'll draw your audience into your performance with imagery.

Hands-On

Unless you're required to have an interactive component for the audience, you may not need to concern yourself with the *Hands-On* learning style. However, if your presentation is something closer to a workshop, you'll want to create a *Tell-Show-Do* element for your presentation. For example, your topic might be *How to Fold the Perfect Paper Airplane*. After you explain the process (*Audible*), you'll demonstrate how to properly fold the paper into an airplane (*Visual*). Then you'll have the audience attempt to fold their own airplane (*Hands-On*). Having first explained the process, then demonstrating how to do it, and finally having the audience fold their own airplane, is a perfect example of incorporating all three learning styles. By following the three steps, the audience will better understand the process, thereby increasing their success rate of creating quality paper airplanes. Address all the learning styles in a *Hands-On* demonstration and you've all but guaranteed your success.

➤The Three Types of Delivery

While there are different ways to display your information, you'll likely find yourself emphasizing your key pieces of information through *Bullet Points* or through *Storytelling*. Both of these approaches work, but deciding on the method should be based on the topic and your speaking style.

Bullet Points
If your presentation is heavy in data or statistics, or you need to emphasize key pieces of information, bullet point lists are a good way to go. In fact, if your assignment requires you to cover specific facts in order to receive full credit, bullet points are the in-your-face approach to ensuring the information has been delivered. They're also a useful tool for your audience if they want to take notes, since bullet points act as

an outline of your presentation. But be careful! Bullet point lists are a tool and not a presentation in and of themselves. They should only reveal a key point. It's your job to fill in the rest of the information as you speak. Use them as needed, but avoid creating thirty slides filled with dots and data. Insert some graphs, pictures, videos, and stories in order to break up the monotony.

Stories
The storytelling approach works well if you're recounting an event or trying to compel your audience to take your position on an issue. And when I say storytelling, I mean a combination of you telling your audience about your topic and allowing your PowerPoint to act as a visual supplement. I liken the storytelling approach to reading a children's book aloud. The reader is telling the story and the book contains a few pictures that supplement what the reader is saying.

Actually, storytelling works with almost any topic that doesn't require the delivery of raw data, such as financials, statistics, percentages, comparisons, or lists. However, since the story approach typically lacks large amounts of data to fill your slides with, you may find it difficult to decide what to put into your presentation. Don't worry if your presentation feels like it's lacking the content needed to fill a minimal number of slides. Your storytelling skills will make up for a lack of projected imagery. I would much rather you have a few good slides and a great story, than a bunch of slides filled with meaningless content.

A Combo Approach
Don't be afraid to combine the bullet point and storytelling approach together. There's no reason that you can't have the stories and the data supplement each other. This is your presentation and your job is to present the information in a manner that makes sense. If at any time you're not sure

which method to use or whether you should combine them, ask yourself, "How can I best convey my message so my audience understands what I'm trying to say?"

CHAPTER 10
How to Create Kick Ass Content

Outside of introducing yourself, you'll want to come up with an opener to your presentation that will grab attention. This is the critical point in which you reach out and convince the crowd that what you're about to say is worth their time. This is the equivalent of grabbing your audience by the shirt collar and saying, "Come with me, you're gonna want to see this." Without a *hook*, you risk leaving the audience to figure out on their own whether they should be interested in your presentation. You need to convince them you have something important to say and that it's worth their time to listen.

➤Start with an Explosion

As an example of a rather unique opener, I had the opportunity to do a series of presentations related to my previous work as a Crime Scene Investigator. I opened with a video that I shot during a training course on how to document explosions and bombing scenes.

The video showed an explosive-filled Toyota Camry sitting all alone in a field. With the push of a button, the explosion ripped the car's roof completely off and launched it well over 100 feet in the air. My classmates and I can be heard on the video giggling in the background at the excitement of having annihilated a junked car. Seconds later, the roof of the car unexpectedly fell back into the camera's view as it returned to earth. More clearly than the sound of the explosion itself is our instructor, who can be heard on the video proclaiming, "Ooooh Shit!", as the roof smashed back onto the car. While my audience laughed at the unexpected comment by my instructor, I promised them I would later show close-up pictures of the devastation and an explanation why this training was an important part of my work. That was my hook, first an explosion, then a promise to show the devastation in more detail towards the end of my presentation.

Okay, so exploding cars may be a bit over the top for most presentations. That doesn't mean that you can't come up with something really cool that will make your audience put down their smart phones and pay attention. I encourage you to be creative, but, if you find yourself stuck, I have four sure-fire methods for getting the job done.

We'll call these attention grabbing openers:

- The Question
- The Promise
- The Unfinished Story
- The Fascinating Facts

All four of these techniques work on the same premise. You're letting your audience know that you'll be providing them with information they simply can't pass up. That's your hook. Here are some examples of how these "hooks" can work for you.

The Question

When asking your audience a question, keep in mind that the question is meant to be thought provoking. The remainder of your presentation will provide your audience with the answer to the question.

Topic: *Benefits of Organic Vegetables*

"Have you ever stood in a grocery store and wondered if the price of vegetables marked *'organic'* was worth the extra cost?"

Topic: *An Argument for Free College*

"Ask yourself, What would be the advantage to this country if every person who wanted it could be provided with a college education at no cost?"

Topic: *The Future of Transportation*

"How many of you wish that you could cut your commute time to work or school in half?"

The Promise

This approach can be presented as either a question or a statement. While similar to asking a question as previously described, your hook will be the promise of providing some critical knowledge your audience will want. You may recognize this method, since it's frequently used in advertising.

Topic: *The World's Next Currency*

"What if I told you that a new form of currency is available that will virtually eliminate the way we pay for goods and services today?"

Topic: *Chocolate Chip Cookies to Die For*

"In the next fifteen minutes, I will give you the secret to making the best chocolate chip cookies in the world."

Topic: *Gambling For Fun and Profit*

"I will teach you a little-known trick that can improve your chances of winning any casino card game by 30 percent."

The Unfinished Story

This technique is equivalent to a movie style cliffhanger. You start off your presentation with a compelling story that leads into what most certainly will be a fascinating conclusion. But right when you're about to get to the good part, you cut the story short and transition into the core of your presentation. You'll of course need to ensure the crowd that you'll return with the conclusion of the story in good time. Make sure that your story is relevant to the topic of your presentation. The following example is fictitious. Make sure that your story is not!

Topic: *Start-Ups for the Fiscally Challenged*

"In Seattle, Washington, three teams of University students were given 1000 dollars each. Their mission? Use this money to create a unique start-up business that generated a profit. The catch? They had just four weeks to complete the task. At the end of the four weeks, the team generating the most income was given the opportunity to pitch their business idea to a major venture capital firm in the Seattle area. At the end of the competition, two of the three teams turned a profit. However, to the surprise of everyone, using a never before seen marketing idea, one of the teams managed to turn a profit of over 100,000 dollars. And after a meeting with the venture capital firm, their product has since generated over 150,000,000 dollars. I will tell you the name of the product later. But first, let me describe why the students were so successful."

Without mentioning the name of the product, you'll go on with your presentation and give the audience all your insights into starting up a business. Once all the teaching points have been covered, remind your audience where you left off in your story and finish it up with the cliffhanger information. In this case, that information is the name of the product that resulted in the massive sales.

The *Unfinished Story* technique can be used with practically any topic. Be sure your story has a compelling conclusion you can hold back until the very end of your presentation.

The Fascinating Facts

Who doesn't love fascinating facts? This technique will pique your audience's attention by providing them with previously unknown, yet interesting bits of information. The Fascinating Facts can be presented as either a statement or a question, and there's no reason to limit yourself to just one fact.

Topic: "The History of Flight"

Fascinating Fact: "In 1903 the Wright Brothers were the first to take to the skies. However, just sixty-six years later, man landed on the moon."

Topic: "The Hidden Secrets in Film"

Fascinating Fact: "If you had been paying attention, you might have noticed that all the clocks in the movie *Pulp Fiction* were set to 4:20."

Topic: "The Standard American Diet"

Fascinating Fact: "Did you know that the average American

drinks over six hundred sodas each year?"

While the four techniques I've described here can work beautifully on their own, keep in mind that nothing prevents you from customizing your hook to fit your needs. For example, consider using a photograph, a video, text on the screen, or some other prop to supplement what it is you're saying. It's been often said, you've got one shot at a first impression! Be creative and convince everyone in the room that what you have to say is going to be awesome.

CHAPTER 11
How Many Slides Should I Create?

If you're looking for a question that has no answer, this is it. There are too many variables to predetermine the number of PowerPoint slides you'll need for the amount of presentation time you will have. In fact, this question would yield a better result if it were asked in reverse. You shouldn't be asking how many slides you should create, but rather how long will it take to go through the slides you've created.

Here's why:

Take your very first slide for example. You may have some basic information on it such as your name and the title of your presentation.

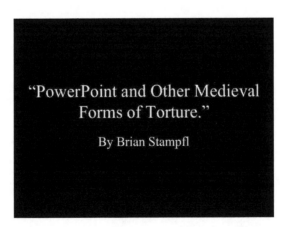

How long is it going to take to introduce yourself and say the title of your presentation? Seven-seconds? Five-seconds? My guess is that you won't be spending tons of time on this slide. If we tried to create a formula for how long each slide should take, we already know that the introductory slide will go faster than all the others. Let's move on to the second slide, which contains an attention grabbing fact, and see how much time it might take.

Put an opening statement like this up on the screen and the audience is going to take notice. But opening statements require context and this is where the speaker will need to take some time to further introduce the topic. How long will it take to get through this slide? Thirty-seconds? A full minute? Several minutes?

Let's take a look at a set of bullet points and see if things smooth out for us.

Death by PowerPoint
Signs and Symptoms

• Eyes Glazed Over

Death by PowerPoint
Signs and Symptoms

• Eyes Glazed Over
• Yawning

Death by PowerPoint
Signs and Symptoms

• Eyes Glazed Over
• Yawning
• Uncontrollable Crying

There are three points (signs and symptoms) being addressed in the slides above. Again, depending on what and how much you have to say about each of these points, the amount of time to cover them will vary. Calculations can get even more complicated depending on how the above bullet list was created. Is it three bullet points spread out over three slides, or is it one slide in which three bullet points appear sequentially?

When I create presentations, I prefer to load the slides with photographs using as little text as possible. The benefit of this approach is that as you're presenting, you can vary the amount of time you spend on each slide. You can talk as much or as little as you want when displaying a picture. This is a useful tactic that will allow you to adjust your presentation on the fly in order to either fill your allotted time or cut back if you're running long. The audience will never know how much time you intended to devote to describing a photograph. However, you don't enjoy the same flexibility with loads of bullet points or other blocks of text. When the audience sees words on the screen, they'll be expecting an explanation. This makes varying the amount of time for that slide more difficult. These are things to consider when deciding how many slides you should have.

My recommendation is to create your content first, then practice for time. If you're running long, delete some of the information. If you're running short, expand on your explanations or add more interesting content. Like I said, there is no preset formula.

➤Just Tell Me How Many Slides I Need!

Okay, fine. But first I need to drive home a few points so that you don't get discouraged if my formula doesn't work out perfectly.

This is a guideline, not a rule. This will help you to start your project, but your final slide count will be based on how much information you have. Don't feel forced into creating slides when you don't have the content, and don't think you have to cut out content based merely on this formula.

Depending on your topic and whether or not you have videos or photos, it's entirely possible that you could create a simple presentation with just five slides. And that's okay! The reverse is true and you may have tons of pictures and videos to show, resulting in a large number of slides. The problem is estimating how many slides you'll need for the amount of content you have.

So here you go, the magic formula:

One Slide For Each Minute You Have To Speak

An amazing formula, I know. So, what are the variables?

- Pace at which you speak
- Number and length of videos
- Number of pictures
- Amount of content

What I've found is that despite the varying amount of time I'll spend on each slide, it tends to average out to about one minute per slide. For example, my first slide, which introduces the name of the presentation, will only require a few seconds of viewing. But a photograph may take longer because it requires some explanation. And a video will take as long as the clip length you plan to show. *One slide for each minute* is simply an average based on my experience. And I've found that the longer the presentation, the more accurate the *one slide for each minute* formula is.

A Word of Warning
If you expect to answer questions during your presentation, you must take this into account when calculating the number of slides you'll need. If you're expecting ten minutes of questions from the audience during a thirty minute presentation, then your actual presentation will likely be closer to twenty minutes long. However, if you're not sure whether or not your audience will ask questions, then I recommend that your presentation be long enough to fill the allotted time. It's easier to cut the audience off from questions than to stand there with ten minutes left and nothing to say.

➤How Long is This Build Going to Take?

In short, a lot longer than you think. I recently completed a 34-slide PowerPoint presentation. I used the exact same guidelines I've presented in this book, and I only had text and photographs to contend with, no video. Despite my experience with preparing presentations, it took me almost six hours to complete the presentation to my liking, and I was in a hurry.

I can hear you now. "Six hours? But why? Why should something so simple take this much time?"

If you're a perfectionist (I am) and want your presentation to stand out, here's a partial list of things to consider when building your masterpiece.

- What's My Topic?
- What Does My Framework Look Like?
- Background Choice

- Font Choice, Size, and Color
- Object Alignment
- Consistent Size of Objects
- Story Flow
- Spelling and Grammar
- Photographs and File Size
- Video Usage

If you're working towards creating a great project, take a guess how long you think you'll need to build your presentation. Now, whatever amount of time you've predicted, multiply it by three. So, if you've predicted that you'll finish in one hour, figure that you'll really need three hours. I'm not trying to stress you out, it's just a fact of life. If you think you can do it in one hour, it'll take three. *Be prepared to put in the time.*

CHAPTER 12
Building the Framework

One of the nice features of PowerPoint is that it allows you to create as many blank slides as you want. Once you populate the slides with pictures, videos, or text, you can easily rearrange the order of the slides. This makes building the presentation easier since you don't have to import your information into the slides in the order that you plan to display them.

Here's the steps I recommend to quickly import your information and get the "framework" of your presentation built. Once you've imported all your information, the rest is just fine-tuning.

Step One:
Create a folder on your computer that contains all of your pictures, logos, videos, and a copy of your outline. This should be in the same folder that your PowerPoint master file is saved. Importing all the information from one place makes things easier.

Step Two:
In PowerPoint, create as many blank slides as you need. Don't worry about making too many or not enough. With two clicks, you can add or delete slides as needed. Notice that you have the option of choosing slides that come preinstalled with text, image, and media boxes in a variety of formats. You can use these pre-formatted slides for a fast and consistent way to lay out your slides, or you can choose the blank slide and customize it as you see fit. If you go with the pre-formatted version, you can delete or modify any part of the

template as needed.

Step Three:
Import all your photos. Don't worry about the order in which you bring them in, and don't worry about sizing or fine-tuning right now. Just get them into the slides.

Step Four:
Import your video. Make sure that the original video is stored and remains in the same folder on your computer as described in Step 1. PowerPoint needs to link back to the original video in order to play properly.

Step Five:
If you've created an outline as I've suggested, simply copy and paste the lines of text from the outline into each slide. If the new slides you've created already have a text box, paste your text into the box. If not, you can use the text tool to define where you want your text to go on the slide. Don't worry about perfect placement right now. The text can be easily moved and modified at any time.

Step Six:
Arrange the slides in the order you plan to display them.

That's the Framework
All of the visual components of your presentation should be imported into slides. The next step is to revisit each slide and fine-tune them so that they have the correct font, color, picture alignment, and all the other details that we'll cover in the next section.

As you make these final adjustments, it's likely that you'll find yourself editing your own work. That is, you'll end up tweaking your text for something that sounds better. You may come up with better ideas how you can convey your message, either by changing the order in which you present your information or by bringing in photos you had not previously considered. Creativity can really kick in at this point in the process. I've personally found that my best ideas came to me while I was fine tuning what I thought was my final product.

Once you're happy with each slide and the order in which they're arranged, delete any extra slides you may have and relax. Your PowerPoint presentation is complete!

➤The Layout

You'll soon be projecting onto a large screen what will likely be the most visible part of your performance. And while I previously stated that your PowerPoint is not your presentation, it's the part of the presentation where errors and bonehead mistakes will be most visible.

I can assure you that if while you're speaking and you slip up, the audience will likely forgive you. In fact, they may not even take notice. Why? Because making errors when speaking is normal. If you handle the error properly, whether it's an unexpected pause, mispronunciation, or a do-over, it will be interpreted as normal speech. However, if you project misspelled words, fuzzy images, or some other easily-corrected mistake onto the screen, and the audience will spot it in a second! Since they'll presume that you had plenty of time to proofread and review your presentation ahead of time, even minor errors will be viewed as irresponsible on your part. Let's avoid that, shall we?

This next section may be the most important part of our PowerPoint discussion. I'll show you how to avoid the most common mistakes that gave meaning to the term *Death by PowerPoint*. And the good news is that it's surprisingly easy to do. Just keep reading, follow my advice, and be assured your presentation is going to look great.

CHAPTER 13
Text

The reality for any presentation is that somewhere along the way, words are going to show up on the screen. It's your job to ensure that those words propel your presentation forward and do not become a distraction for your audience.

As an example of a very common distraction, I've seen on numerous occasions presentations in which journal articles were pasted into a slide. This was of course followed up by the presenter reading the article to the audience. There is no crueler joke to play. DO NOT paste large blocks of text into your presentation. No audience wants to read a book projected on a screen.

To correct this problem, I subscribe to the theory that *less is more* when it comes to text. Think of text not as a way to convey information to your audience, but as visual cues and reminders of the information you're sharing with them.

As a means of comparison, take a look at the following bullet point list detailing the major benefits of recycling. This is not an unusual amount of content for the average presenter to convey on a single slide.

- *Recycling will help reduce the size of landfills by eliminating 75% of consumer waste including glass, plastics, paper, and other household items. These recyclable items could then be reused rather than piling up on land.*

- *Recycling programs create job opportunities for this new and growing industry. Once the items are received at the recycle facility, they are sorted by hand by hundreds of employees throughout the country so that the items may be shipped to their final destination.*

- *Recycling helps to conserve natural resources by reusing items that are commonly thrown away. Prior to recycling programs, companies drew from natural resources to replace those items, such as the cutting down of trees to make paper. Recycling of paper alone is estimated to save over 250 million trees each year!*

While the information about recycling in the example above is accurate, there's just too much of it. The audience is not going to want to read entire passages about recycling. If by chance someone does start reading it, they're going to become conflicted when you start talking.

Consider again the *less is more* theory. Take a look at how the same three benefits of recycling can be conveyed in just a few words.

- *Reduce Landfill*
- *Create Jobs*
- *Conserve Resources*

Notice there aren't any complete sentences above, just a few words to convey the point. I can promise you as an audience member, I'd much rather see the shorter bullet point version than the longer one. That frees me up to assess what you're speaking about, and then allows me to listen to you rather than being forced to read. Remember, your presentation is about you conveying the information as a speaker. The PowerPoint and what's contained inside is designed to *support* you, not *carry* you!

➤Font Choice

Want to make your audience squint? Use an unreadable font.

I've had debates about what is the best font to use for PowerPoint presentations. In my opinion, deciding on a font is a no-brainer. Simply pick a font that's easy to read. I would recommend using the same fonts you'd likely use when submitting a paper, such as Times New Roman, Arial, or Helvetica.

If you're interested in creating a stylistic look to your presentation and want to use a fancy font, consider using it sparingly. You could certainly spruce up your introductory slides that list your name and presentation title. You may have other slides that are less critical components of your presentation, and no one is going to mind an artistic enhancement to those. But everything else should be considered an important part of your delivery, and your audience deserves to easily read what you've written.

Lastly, if you have a master slide template that contains a header, a footer, or some logo that you're going to display throughout the presentation, feel free to be creative in this design. I still recommend that anything you put into the master slide be easy to read and recognize. But since this may be more of a design element, a creative touch won't hurt.

➤Font Color

The easiest color combination to read is black text on a white background. The moment you begin to change the font color to anything else, the contrast between the font and the background changes and it can be harder to read. That's not to say that you can't use colored fonts. You just want to be sure that they're readable to your audience.

For example, most dark colored fonts should work well on a white background. However, a yellow font on white is a miserable choice and will be practically unreadable.

The second best combination, and the one that I use most often, is white text on a black background. One of the advantages of using a black or dark background is that when your presentation is projected, there isn't as much reflection from the screen. Depending on the size of the screen and how close your audience is sitting, the reflection can actually light up the front row and create an uncomfortable glare. Projecting a dark background reduces this problem.

Keep in mind if you add color to your fonts while on a dark background the readability will begin to decrease. I've found that a yellow font on a black background is about as much contrast as I'm comfortable with. And then after some further consideration, I usually resort back to a white font. But whatever color combinations you choose, you'll want to test it on a projected screen to make sure it's readable and looks good.

And lastly, avoid giving each letter in a sentence a different color. If you do that, your presentation will look as if created by a child. Don't do that!

➤Font Size

Your font needs to be large enough for your audience to read. What you're able to read on your computer screen may not be easy for your audience to read. Consider that there may be several rows of audience members. No one in your audience is going to be as close to the projected screen as you are to your computer screen. Those poor folks in the back row may have a tough time reading smaller text. And with an older audience, this factor multiplies.

There's no straightforward formula for what size font to choose. Start with what looks good on your computer screen, but don't be afraid to use the space you have. Hopefully, you'll be able to test your presentation beforehand. When you do, stand at the furthest distance from the screen that your audience will be seated. If the fonts are hard to read, bump up their size until they look good. This is a quick and easy fix, one that's worth your time.

➤Spelling and Grammar

If you project a misspelled word onto a huge screen, be assured that your audience will notice it. Discovering the mistake yourself while actually presenting will likely cause your heart to skip a beat. Although not the end of the world, who needs the drama?

Luckily, PowerPoint has a spell checker built in. As you type, words that are spelled incorrectly will be underlined with a red dotted line, similar to when working in Microsoft Word™[1]. Presuming that you've used the correct word (e.g., Your vs. You're), there really shouldn't be any reason to have misspellings.

Grammar is a different animal and PowerPoint does not make suggestions regarding sentence structure. If you've followed my recommended guidelines of using a minimal amount of text and avoiding complete sentences when creating bullet points, grammar most likely won't be a problem. But no matter what you create, double check your work, and have a friend proofread your work as well. One of you is bound to find an easily correctable mistake.

[1] Microsoft Word™ is a trademark of Microsoft Corporation.

CHAPTER 14
Photograph File Size and Resolution

For presentations containing more than about five photographs, you'll want to pay attention to file size. PowerPoint can get bogged down when you load it up with large files. You will see the file size dilemma creep up on you when you are building your presentation. As you periodically hit the save button, each save cycle will take longer following the addition of large photo files. This longer save time can cost you over the long run when you don't use appropriately-sized photos. You'll also find that the presentation can take longer to launch, and you'll be more prone to crashes.

Your best bet is to adjust the images resolution so that the longest dimension is around 1024 pixels. The shorter dimension will fall where it will depending on the aspect ratio. This can be done with any photo editing software and even within PowerPoint itself. This is a common resolution size for both computers and projectors, and the file size created at this resolution will be a manageable one.

➤Picture Quality

Use high quality photos in your presentation. A blurry, pixelated, or otherwise poor looking photo on your computer screen will look twice as bad on a projected screen. The only exception would be if the image you are showing is an important part of your presentation and is of poor quality to begin with. For example, there are pictures available of Bigfoot and the Loch Ness Monster. You'll notice that all the pictures are really bad. Strangely, it's the poor quality of those same pictures that helps to keep the mystique and mystery alive. In my example, they would be appropriate for use.

A more likely example would be photos taken during World War I. Your source photo may be damaged in some manner, have a soft focus or some other defect that is out of your control. But in these instances, it's those very flaws that make the photo special and therefore completely acceptable for presentation use. But if your pictures have been taken either by you or by some current source, make sure they're top-notch.

As a side note, many schools and businesses are switching from projector systems to large, high-definition flat panel displays. If you're fortunate enough to be able to use a flat panel display rather than a projected image, you'll really want to ensure that your images are high quality. The brightness and clarity of a flat panel screen will make any sub-par images even worse.

➤Screen Brightness

This is an important point to pay attention to, especially if you've included photographs in your presentation. As you build your presentation, your photographs will appear crisp and bright on the computer screen. Excluding high-end projector systems or flat panel displays, most projectors don't have the power to display your presentation with the same brightness as your computer screen. Your photographs will appear darker on the projected screen than they will on your computer monitor.

Brightness is a common problem and most often discovered during the actual presentation itself. On several occasions, I've stood dumbfounded by the poor quality of the picture projected onto the big screen. All I could do was assure the crowd that if they could see my computer screen, they'd be impressed by how beautiful my photographs were. These were embarrassing moments to be sure.

Luckily, this problem can be avoided by brightening up the photos. In PowerPoint, you'll be able to make adjustments to your photographs, including the brightness. I've found that increasing the brightness by 10-15% generally fixes the problem. Your results may vary depending on the quality of the photo to start with. Again, if the equipment you'll be using is of a good quality, this may not be necessary but it probably won't hurt either. It's better to have a brighter image that can be seen than a dark one that cannot.

➤Highlighting Details on a Picture

You might find that there's a detail within a slide that you'll want to draw attention to. I often find this to be true with photographs. Rather than trying to verbally describe to your audience where to look, or stand in front of the screen and point, you can insert objects such as circles or arrows into your slide to highlight the detail you want your audience to focus on.

Let's say you have a picture of a car. You want to show your audience the car first, but then want to draw their attention to the left headlight. PowerPoint has a variety of shapes that can be inserted into your slide. In this case, I'd suggest a circle big enough to encompass the headlight, with a line thickness that can easily be seen. Next, I'd choose a color for the circle that has a good contrast to the background image. Red and yellow tend to stand out most of the time.

As you're advancing your slides, the picture of the car will appear, and you can describe whatever you need to about the car. When you advance the slide again, the circle will appear, drawing the audience's attention to the headlight. This method looks clean and shows that you were prepared to talk about a specific detail of the bigger subject. You didn't have to struggle with explaining where the audience should look, or try to point out the details. The circle that you placed on the slide did it for you.

By the way, there are two ways to have an object, such as a circle, appear on your photograph. Let's go back to the car and the red circle around the headlight example. The first way is to create a slide with the photograph of the car, then use the *Duplicate* command in PowerPoint to create an exact duplicate of the first slide. Place the red circle around the headlight on the second of the two slides. As you advance through your slides, the picture of the car will appear. When you advance again, the second picture of the car will appear with the circle around the headlight. This method looks seamless and is the easiest way to do it.

The second method is to create just one slide that will contain both the photograph of the car and the red circle. You will use the *Animation* feature (not otherwise recommended) to "instruct" the red circle to appear on the picture of the car when you advance the slide. As you advance through your slides, you will come to the picture of the car. When you hit the advance button again, the slide *will not* actually advance. Instead, the advance button activates the arrival of the red circle. It looks exactly the same as the previously mentioned method, but the process is slightly more involved.

While either of these methods will work, there may be an advantage to using the second method, especially if you're creating a large presentation. By creating only one slide with the picture of the car, you reduce total file size.

CHAPTER 15
Video

There's no question in my mind that video creates the most problems for presenters of all levels. I've personally screwed up the insertion, linking, and transfer of video in PowerPoint so many times that I'm leery of using it. But it does work, if you know what you're doing.

Having relevant video in your presentation can be awesome. Audiences respond well to video and it can add one more dimension to your presentation, and give you a short break from speaking. While I will have to refer you to your online manual and other resources for learning how to embed video correctly into your presentation software, here are the top four ways that video can kill your presentation:

1) Poor Quality - Your video needs to be of a good quality and have good sound. Whether you pull the video off the internet or create the video using your iPhone, it has to look like the person who created it took care in doing so. Watch out for poor lighting, jerky movements or poor sound quality. Show an inferior video and you'll have an inferior presentation.

2) Lost In Transfer - When you create your presentation, PowerPoint will give you the option of linking your video to a slide. This function is extremely easy and the video should work brilliantly on the computer you're working on. It's when you transfer your presentation to a thumb drive, CD, or other media that you run into problems.

Here is an explanation of the problem with media transfer

for video files. When PowerPoint links the video into the slide, the impression you get is that the video file has been copied into your PowerPoint file. This is not the case. PowerPoint is only linking itself to the video file stored somewhere else on your computer. So, when you copy your PowerPoint presentation file to your thumb drive or CD, you're actually leaving the video file behind. When you run your presentation on a different computer, PowerPoint will try to locate the file, but there will be nothing for it to find and play!

In order to avoid the "lost" video problem I mentioned, create a unique folder for your PowerPoint presentation. Drag your video file into this same folder before linking the video file into your PowerPoint slide. When you transfer your presentation to your thumb drive or CD, copy the entire folder containing all the files you've used to create the presentation. This can be done, specifically in PowerPoint for the PC, by using the save function called *Package for CD*. This critical function ensures that all the linked materials are transferred to your thumb drive or CD.

Lastly, no matter how confident you are of your file transfer, test to see that your PowerPoint presentation works on a computer other than the one you created it on. *I promise that if you're going to have problems with video, it will most likely occur when you transfer your presentation to a thumb drive or other media and move to another computer. I can't emphasize this enough!!!*

3) Linking Problems - It's possible to create links within your slides that will allow you to access videos through the internet. You click the link and PowerPoint accesses the website and plays the video of your choice. If you choose to go this route, once again, do your testing. Having a reliable internet connection and websites that don't play well when I need them to are risky variables. This method can work, but proceed with caution.

4) Not Embedding Videos - If you want to come off like a complete amateur, give this a try. Don't link your video into your presentation. Just exit PowerPoint each time you want to play a video, search for the video file, and launch the video using whatever player happens to open up. Then when you're done with the video, close it, re-launch PowerPoint, find where you left off and continue on.

I've seen this method used many times, and each time I was convinced I was watching a novice. Take the time to link the videos correctly. Your audience will appreciate it.

CHAPTER 16
Transitions and Animations

If you've skimmed over everything up to this point, this is where you will find the cash value of this book. Here you either go pro or go home. And I can sum it up in one sentence:

No Amount of Smoke and Mirrors Can Make Up for Bad Content.

PowerPoint is a powerful program filled with tons of features. However, there are two drop-down menus that once accessed, will take you down the road to purgatory. In this bad trip, you'll begin creating visual spectacles of vomit-inducing horror that seriously contribute to *Death by PowerPoint*!

How can you make your presentation ten times better than your classmates? Avoid using the Transitions and Animation features.

Transitions
Transitions are how PowerPoint *visually* handles the changes between slides as you advance through them. The default transition is for the currently viewed slide to simply disappear and the new one appear, each time you advance the slide. It's simple and completely acceptable. However, fill your presentation with the thirty-five or so available transitions, and you're guaranteed to ruin someone's life!

While I could try to explain some of the transitions available, I'll just give you some of the names for them. Under

PowerPoint's own submenu of *Exciting*, there's the *Honeycomb*, *Vortex*, and *Shred*. Under the submenu of *Dynamic Content* there's the *Ferris Wheel*, *Fly-Through*, and *Orbit*. These are fabulous, three-dimensional, flipping, turning, mind-bending effects that work great, that is if you want to trick your audience into thinking you have content.

Exception Alert! While I just got through implying you are forbidden to use the transitions in PowerPoint, there is one transition, if you choose it, will not cause me to mock you. The *Fade Transition* is a smooth transition that allows the currently viewed slide to fade out and the new slide to fade into view. You can even choose the amount of time the transition takes.

The benefit of this transition is that it takes away the abruptness of having the slides snap into view. This is a judgment call, but I've found that the fade works well with presentations that have a calm or low-key tone to them. For example, if your presentation was on *Stress Reduction Techniques*, *Caring for Disabled Veterans*, or *Solutions for Sleep Disorders*, then Fade is a good choice.

Animations

PowerPoint allows you to take any text, picture, icon, or whatever you can stuff into a slide and animate it in hundreds of different ways. For example, if you want the text to perform a stunt as it appears, you can make it spin, swirl, or tumble onto the screen. If you have a photograph, you can make it bounce onto the screen and continue to bounce in progressively smaller steps.

It gets worse...

PowerPoint has animation options for anything that enters onto the screen, options for once it has arrived, and for the same text or object when it finally leaves the screen.

But Why Are Transitions and Animations Bad?

Simply stated - Transitions and Animations serve no real purpose and often become an annoying distraction.

Keep in mind what it is you're trying to do when giving a presentation. Are you:

- Defending a thesis and need to convince a panel your research is complete and your conclusion sound?

- Giving biographical information on someone famous?

- Compelling the audience to take your position on a specific topic?

- Providing training to your audience?

- Describing a process or providing instruction of some sort?

- Making a comparison between two financial investment strategies?

No matter what your topic, I'm guessing that having your text do cartwheels across the screen is not going to improve the quality of your presentation or impress your audience.

Enough said.

CHAPTER 17
Object Alignment

This is a pro-level tip, but one that will keep your audience from tilting their heads trying to figure out what's not quite right about your presentation.

When you advance your slides in PowerPoint, one screen disappears and the next one appears instantly. If you happen to have the same text showing up consecutively on several slides, such as a header or the title of the section you're currently speaking about, it's important that the text is in the exact same place on each slide. If not, when you advance the slide, the text will appear to have jumped to its new location. The jump may slight, but it will be noticeable. After several slide advances, the text will appear to have been hopping around the slides, and will signal to the audience that you have no idea what you're doing.

The same thing goes for logos, pictures, or other objects that you may be showing on several consecutive slides. Make sure that the object or text is the same size and in the same position each time. If you're using a variety of photographs, when possible, make them all the same size on the screen. If the pictures must be different sizes, then position them so that each one is centered on the slide. If this is not possible, or if you have multiple pictures on each slide, position them so that the pictures on each subsequent slide share a common border. This means they are aligned at either the top or bottom, left or right. This will make the transitions between pictures appear smoother and less distracting.

There are a variety of ways to ensure everything is

aligned. If you have just a few slides, you can "eyeball" everything into position. Then you can click between the slides making adjustments as needed until everything appears lined up. This process works but is not very efficient if you have lots of images or text, or more than about five slides.

Rather than eyeballing your text and images into place, consider using PowerPoint's *Guides* and *Snap* options. These menu options will assist you in aligning your objects automatically. There are also some visual aids, consisting of lines and grids, which are superimposed over the slide to give you a visual reference while trying to lay out the contents of your slide.

If you plan on having the same text, like a header or a logo, on the majority of your slides, I'd recommend you create a Master Slide. In PowerPoint, you create one slide with the images you want to appear each time. Then each time you create a new slide, the fixed text and images will appear in the same place. You can then add whatever you want to each Master Slide, as you build your presentation.

If you're not familiar with the PowerPoint menu options I've mentioned here, the PowerPoint help menu will walk you through the steps to use them. Use the search terms *Align, Grid, Dynamic Guides*, and *Static Guides* to get started.

➤Visually Balanced

In photography, there's a technique called *Fill the Frame*. When you take a picture, the goal is to have your key subject fill the majority of the space in your image. For example, if you were to take a picture of your friend, you'd want your friend to be up close so that you could see them in the picture. The reverse of this would be if your friend (the prime subject) was way out in the distance and the majority of the image was of the parking lot they were standing in. You should think of your PowerPoint slide design in the same way that you would when composing a quality photograph.

I've already said that text on the screen needs to be big enough so that your audience can read it. It's equally important that images be large enough to see as well. And if you have a combination of both, it's not only important to fill the screen, but to do it in an aesthetically pleasing manner. In short, it needs to look good.

How you accomplish this balance of images, including headers, footers, and text, requires an artistic touch. There is no exact way to do this other than to put what you want in the slide, then move your images and text around until it looks good. You may have to shrink or expand your images and text in order to find the right balance. I've found that the less you have on any individual slide, the easier it is to find this balance. The more images and text you place on a slide will require additional shuffling to see how the pieces fit best.

CHAPTER 18
Relevancy

Once your PowerPoint is filled with everything you think you need, it may be time to remove some non-vital content. While it's possible you may have too much stuff jammed into your presentation, it's also possible you may have the wrong stuff jammed in there too. I've seen many presentations in which the presenter inserted a goofy video, a cartoon, and even pictures of their pets! All of this would've been fine except they had nothing to do with the topic being discussed. Inserting material that's a guaranteed laugh or an "aww" moment ensures a certain amount of feel-good success. All presenters want to please the crowd, but will inserting non-relevant information improve your chances for a better grade?

In my opinion, the reason presenters choose to do this is because they're uncomfortable about the quality of their presentation. The presenter is worried what they have to say is not interesting and they're afraid they might not please the crowd. Apparently inserting a funny cat video may seem like the only way to spruce up a presentation entitled, *The History of the Grapefruit.*

My advice is to avoid putting pictures, jokes, or videos into your presentation just to get a laugh. Instead, realize that if what you've created won't be able to stand on its own merit, it's time to go back and figure out why.

As a first step, it may be worth going back to ensure that you know the material well. Next, revisit your delivery. Are you presenting to the audience or merely talking at them?

Since you're presenting information that your audience most likely knows nothing about, there's no reason that you can't craft a clever delivery. If needed, go back and revisit the section entitled *Studying the Greats - Develop Your Style.* What you'll find is that the topic they're discussing may not be particularly interesting in and of itself. It's the passion, knowledge of the material, and the delivery that makes it worth listening to. And now it's your job to make your material equally as interesting and more relevant than a picture of your pet hamster.

Section 4

Kick Ass List of Extras

CHAPTER 19
Props

Up to this point, the focus has been on knowing your material and building a bulletproof PowerPoint presentation. And as far as I'm concerned, if you've got those two elements down, you're going to be good to go. You'll have a solid presentation, one that you can be proud of. But as I've mentioned earlier, if you want to cross over from good to legendary, you've got to make the leap from "plain ol' speaker" to an actual performer. This is where introducing a prop into the presentation can make a huge difference.

But before you grab just any item to hold up in front of the audience, some thought has to go into the process. What you bring with you and how you use the item will determine whether you've brought a *performance prop* or an item for *show and tell*.

Performance Props

Think of a *performance prop* as yet another means of relaying your message. It can be the focal point of your presentation or tied to your storytelling. It may be that your performance prop is simply a symbol of your presentation's theme. It may be something you hold in your hand, the clothes you wear, or an item set on a table off to the side. But unlike a *show and tell prop*, the performance prop will remain in your control the entire time. And while you may draw attention to the item you're using, you should not have to describe what the item is, for example, *This is my grandfather's Medal of Honor.* It's more subtle than that. A pocket watch that represents time, an empty lunch box that represents families who can't afford to feed their children, a key to represent a breakthrough in technology, a toy train that links together a series of childhood memories. There are no rules for what item you choose. It doesn't have to have a deep personal meaning. It doesn't have to have a sad or happy theme, or convey a specific emotion. The performance prop is a tool, and if your prop works, it becomes an extension of your story.

In the *Studying the Greats - Develop Your Style* section, I mentioned how Robin Williams and Amanda Palmer used performance props as a means to enhance their delivery. Robin Williams used his American Flag patterned shirt to provide a visual image while he spoke about the history of the American Flag. Amanda Palmer stood on a wooden box and held a small flower while recounting her experience as a living statue. Neither the shirt nor the flower of either speaker was particularly interesting. But as props, these items became critical elements of the speaker's storytelling and helped make their performances more powerful.

If you're fortunate enough to be able to incorporate a relevant prop into your performance, the potential impact and added fun is unlimited. But like all aspects of your presentation, you'll need to practice. Don't wait until you're up on stage to figure out how your performance prop will be incorporated into your talk.

How hard could it be to talk with a flower in your hand?
Trust me on this. That flower could become your personal nightmare as you realize there's a huge difference between presenting with a flower in your hand and presenting using a flower. No matter what your performance prop is, knowing ahead of time how you will hold the item, move with it, how you'll introduce it, and even when you might set the item down should all be thought out ahead of time. At a minimum, practice with your performance prop at least once or twice.

You'll thank me later.

And now, something to consider: After all my excitement in telling you how cool performance props are, there will be times when holding a flower or wearing an American Flag shirt may not be appropriate. Performance props are presentation enhancers. However, if your topic is of a serious nature or if you're delivering raw data, knowing your material and having a great PowerPoint presentation may be enough. For example, if you were doing a presentation on fatal childhood diseases, global warming, or some other topic of a sensitive nature, some thought should go into whether a performance prop would be appropriate. A well-chosen performance prop could help to drive the message home. But, too much enthusiasm at the wrong time could be considered irresponsible. You can still be knowledgeable and even enthusiastic. But be careful not to give the impression you're making light of a serious topic. If your presentation is being graded and you're not sure how your prop idea will be received, ask your instructor what he or she thinks. If your presentation doesn't have a grade associated with it, you'll likely have more flexibility to customize your presentation as you see fit. In short, know when to ramp up your performance, and know when to pull back.

Show and Tell Props
Think back to the third grade when teddy bears and favorite toys were the topics of classroom speeches. *Show and tell props* are those items relevant to your topic that you will hold up to the audience and actually describe. These are the types of props where you might actually say something along the lines of, "This is my grandfather's Medal of Honor." The benefit of *show and tell props* is that you can present items to the audience that might otherwise be difficult to describe. Or the item might be so unique or personal that your mere possession of the item makes it special. Regardless of what

your *show and tell prop* is, it's an opportunity to further capture interest of your listeners, enhance their learning, and to make a connection with the crowd. But, there are some things you might need to consider...

While *show and tell props* can be a fantastic addition to your already fantastic presentation, there can be some downsides. As I mentioned with the *performance props*, you'll want to know ahead of time how you'll actually handle the item while you're speaking. For example, do you plan to hold the item up for the audience to see, or will you allow the item to be passed around? Are you bringing in a small coin recovered from the Titanic, and if so, should it be handled by everyone? If you allow the same coin to be passed around to the audience, are you sure you'll get it back?

Prop management can be a pain. However, I have a few suggestions.

I'm a huge proponent of tactical thinking. The more control you have over your presentation, the greater chance of your success. The component of your presentation that you have the least control over is the audience. With that in mind, I do not recommend handing any of your props over to the audience for them to pass around. Here's why:

- Audience attention is drawn away from you

- Private conversations among audience members occur

- Passing of the item is a distraction for you and the audience both

- Your item may be dropped, broken, lost, or stolen

So what do you do if you happen to have a gold coin

recovered from the Titanic that fits perfectly into your presentation? You'd like to share it with the class, but you certainly don't want to pass it around for fear of losing it. For the greatest effect, I'd recommend that you hold the coin up for all to see, but show a close-up photograph of the coin in your PowerPoint presentation. It's a perfect solution. You dazzle the crowd by showing proof of ownership, mitigate the risk and hassles of passing it around, and with a projected image the audience gets to see the details of the coin in high-definition. And whether it's your grandfather's medal, the coin from the Titanic, or your award winning Teacup Poodle, this tactical approach will work with almost any item you choose to make a *show and tell prop*.

A Word of Warning!
If your presentation is to be held at a school of any sort, DO NOT bring weapons, explosives, anything dangerous, or anything that might be perceived as such. This includes firearms, ammunition, knives, swords, throwing stars, nunchuks, spears, dangerous chemicals, and pit bulls. There are no schools that I'm aware of that would appreciate having you bring those things onto campus. Doing so may elicit a response by a SWAT team, followed by very poor treatment and possible criminal charges.

Seriously, leave that stuff at home!

CHAPTER 20
All the Gadgets

➤Remote Control or Keyboard?

Unless there's some technical reason preventing you from doing so, you'll likely be responsible for advancing your PowerPoint slides yourself. This is good since only you will know when you're ready to move on to the next slide. And to this point, I don't recommend having a third party advance your slides for you. I've tried this approach myself, and the flow of my talk was broken each time I paused to signal my assistant to advance the slide. Doing it yourself will keep the timing smooth.

Keyboard - The space bar will move you forward, the backspace key (delete key) will take you back. On some keyboards, the arrow keys work the same way. If you have to use the keyboard to advance your slides, don't feel forced to stand in one place just because the keyboard isn't mobile. Allow yourself to move around, even if it's just to move out from behind the desk, podium, or AV roller cart where the keyboard is stationed.

And on that note: Don't allow the location of the keyboard, at a desk for instance, to lure you into sitting down. Barring a disability, no presentation should be given while sitting on your butt.

Remote Control - This is the best option if you have one available. Remotes allow you to move freely around the room. You won't be forced to stand near the keyboard or find yourself having to run back each time you want to advance the slide. Remotes tend to be small enough to conceal in your hand. And with usually no more than two or three buttons, one for advancing and another for backing up the presentation, not much can go wrong. Well, except for the batteries going dead mid-flight. Having extra batteries on hand is a good idea.

A Word of Warning!
That third button on the remote is often a built-in laser pointer. Please see the *Laser Pointers* section regarding my thoughts on the use of lasers during your presentation. <u>Hint:</u> Don't use it.

If you find that the computer you'll be using doesn't have a remote control, you can purchase one that will work wirelessly through the computer's USB port. They are fairly inexpensive, but may not be a good investment if you don't foresee yourself using it more than once.

➤Microphones and Podiums

If you're in a classroom setting, you're probably not going to need a microphone. But if you're going to be in a larger room, such as a conference room or auditorium, then it may become necessary. I've had many instances where the organizers of the event provided a microphone. But since I speak fairly loudly and can project my voice, I often do not use one. This is a call that you have to make once you size up the room and the crowd. Don't feel obligated to use a microphone. If you can take control of the room with your powerful voice, have at it. But if you decide to use a microphone, there are a few points to keep in mind:

• While this may seem obvious, it's important to know that

microphones are expensive pieces of equipment that must be cared for. Dropping or otherwise abusing them can cause damage and generally piss off the owner. I mention this because I've seen on several occasions comedians intentionally drop the microphone to the floor for comedic effect. Unless you have a prearranged agreement to pay for any damaged equipment, I'd suggest not employing the "mic drop" technique.

- Microphones can be a real hassle if they're mounted to a podium or mic stand. Unless they're removable, you may be restricted in your ability to move around. If possible, I'd suggest removing the microphone from the fixed stand, move out from behind the podium, and enjoy greater movement.

- If you're so lucky as to have a lapel or headset style microphone, this will allow you not only to move around freely, but your hands will remain empty. Typically these types of systems will consist of a pager-sized battery box that will clip onto your belt or somewhere on your clothing. The actual microphone is clipped to your shirt, usually somewhere above chest height. Modern headsets are barely discernible. They wrap around from the back of your head and suspend a small microphone near your mouth. These are commonly used for musicians and professional speakers due to their convenience.

- Since your voice will be amplified through a speaker system, you'll need to be aware of how loud you're speaking. You don't want to blow out everyone's eardrums by yelling into the microphone. On the other hand, realize that using a microphone doesn't mean you can get away with speaking quietly. Hopefully, you'll have a chance to test out the system in advance. If not, your first few sentences to the crowd will be critical in determining how loud you should be speaking (Test Test Testing Test Test).

- When holding the microphone, be careful how closely you bring it to your mouth. I don't know the technical reason for this, but with some microphone systems, when you speak with your mouth too close to the microphone, you create a loud blast of feedback. If this happens, you and everyone in the room will know instantly. Just pull the microphone away from your mouth an inch or two and you should be good.

- Don't let the microphone touch your mouth. Doing so is the equivalent of licking a telephone mouthpiece. Lot's of people will have used the microphone and will have been breathing into it for long periods of time.

➤Laser Pointers

Somewhere along the line, somebody came up with the idea that using a laser pointer to point out details on the screen would be a good idea. It's not!

Here are the problems:

- No matter how hard you try to hold that little red dot still on the screen, your own heartbeat is enough to cause the beam to flutter. The red dot bounces around making it look like the presenter is having a seizure.

- Laser pointers are like eating potato chips. You can't eat just one, and you can't use a laser pointer just one time. I've seen presenters attempt to substitute the laser for a quality presentation. They spend most of their time dazzling the crowd by pointing out insignificant details on their insignificant slides.

- Lasers can cause pain and discomfort when inadvertently shined into the eyes of your audience.

- Using a laser pointer makes you look like a nerd.

➤Where's Technical Support?

I hope that wherever you'll be presenting, the equipment you'll use will be of the highest quality, already set up, and free from all technical glitches. But be assured, while we can hope all we want, it doesn't always turn out that way.

I've had many anxious moments surrounded by an audience waiting for me to troubleshoot equipment that didn't belong to me. This was a common experience when the speaking event was hosted at either a hotel or a country club. Usually a busboy would bring the equipment out on a rolling cart, a mixture of loose cables and parts, made available to any business group using the facility. If a problem came up, there was never a person at the hotel who had any knowledge of the equipment, or could answer the simple question, "Where's the power cord?" And since the equipment was unfamiliar, I'd often spend what seemed like hours just figuring out how to set up and turn on the projector.

While I don't expect that you'll have to concern yourself with troubleshooting unfamiliar equipment, it's good to keep in mind that if you do run into technical trouble, you may have to figure it out for yourself. Luckily, if you're in a classroom setting, you may receive assistance from your teacher or another student. If you're at a hotel or country club, you may have to ask the busboy.

I may have mentioned this a few times already, but if you have the chance to test out the equipment and your presentation ahead of time, do it! Because when you call for technical support, they might not answer.

CHAPTER 21
Room Configuration

If you've ever been to a comedy club, magic show, or performance that required audience participation, you may have noticed that the seating was drawn close together and placed near the performer. There's a reason for this and performance artists know they can benefit from how the seating is arranged. As a presenter, you can use *Room Configuration* to your advantage, as well.

When people are drawn close together, group dynamics begin to kick in. Mob mentality is an example of this phenomenon, where otherwise nice folks take cues from someone acting badly. Before you know it, lots of people are acting badly and a riot breaks out. We want to take advantage of the positive influence people can have on others around them.

If you have any control where your audience will sit, you'll want them as far forward and as close together as possible. If you have a small crowd in a large space, you may have to ask people to move forward, since it's not uncommon for people to want to spread out and sit towards the back. By doing so, you'll improve the odds of a group dynamic occurring. For example, we know that laughter is contagious. When someone in a group of people begins to laugh (hopefully when it's appropriate), those in the immediate area may be inspired to laugh as well. Tell a few good jokes and the likelihood that everyone starts laughing increases. But keep in mind it's not actually laughter you're looking for. What you want with your audience is connection. Laughter is just one benefit of connection which can manifest itself in a variety of ways. It may show up as audience participation, asking questions, and appropriate emotional responses to the information you've provided. Obtaining that connection with your audience is a major key to success. Bringing your audience in physically tighter will allow them to share each other's energy, which can be a benefit to you.

If you have the ability to arrange chairs ahead of time in the venue where you'll be speaking, by all means, do so. If you plan to speak in an auditorium setting where the seats are bolted to the floor, arrive early and invite the audience members to sit up close so that they can see the cool stuff you have to show them. If that nonconformist kid from your class sits in the back of the room with his feet on the table, tell him he's gonna have to suck it up and join the rest of the class. It's your show. Take control and make it work for you.

Of course, all this seating customization may not be possible every time. You may not have the option of directing people where to sit, or they just may not move. Don't worry about it. I've actually had great connections with people who've sat at the rear of relatively empty auditoriums. You may just have to work a bit harder. But if your material is good, the connections will come.

➤Lights On or Off?

The short answer is, it depends. If the projector you use for your PowerPoint presentation projects a bright and crisp image, you may be able to do your presentation with the lights on. However, older projectors with aging bulbs may not pump out enough light to produce a satisfactory image it a lit room.

I prefer turning the majority of the lights off during my

presentations to ensure that the screen image is not washed out, regardless of the projector quality. I leave a few lights on that are not directly above the screen so that anyone taking notes or moving around the room will be able to see.

There's one small disadvantage to turning off lights while you're speaking. It seems for some people, just a bit of darkness and a warm room can trigger unscheduled naps. I've watched audience members as their heads bobbed back and forth while they fought to stay awake (actually, these were mostly my students). I've yet to have anyone go into a deep sleep accompanied by snoring, but it's disconcerting to watch from stage while someone is going in and out of consciousness. If this happens while you're speaking, don't take it personally. Just keep going.

➤Handouts

If you're thinking about distributing some sort of handout to your audience, I have a few recommendations. First, make sure that the process of getting the paperwork, or whatever you plan on handing out, doesn't become a distraction. I recommend passing out your paperwork prior to starting your presentation and not in the middle. Taking a break to pass stuff out kills your flow and usually takes longer than expected. Once the process is complete, you'll have to work to recapture audience attention, as they will have been chatting with their neighbors and glancing at their cell phones. Don't give them that opportunity!

When creating your handouts, produce the minimum number of pages possible and staple multiple pages together. This reduces the risk of pages getting dropped or someone not getting the correct number of pages. When passing them out, think tactically and ask yourself how you can best distribute your handouts in the most efficient way. If you have a small group of people, distribute them yourself, making sure to say hello to each person you come in contact with. This is a great time to begin making a connection with audience members, and I've found that speaking with people ahead of time helps eliminate some of my nervousness. If the audience is large, personal delivery may not be practical. Just give several people a portion of your handouts, telling them to take one and pass on the rest. There's no reason not to put your audience to work.

Anticipate the possibility that someone may walk in late after you've already begun talking. Decide ahead of time if you're going to want to stop talking so you can walk over and deliver a handout to the latecomer. Generally speaking, unless the information you have to pass out is critical to the ability to experience your presentation, ignore the late guy and just keep speaking. He or she can pick up the materials from you when the session is done.

While we're on the subject of handouts, take a moment to think about whether they're a necessary part of your presentation. If your presentation is a one shot deal for a grade, and you think that handing out some information to the class will add value, then go for it. But if you plan on presenting the same topic several times to different groups, you may want to reconsider. The problem with handouts is that printing can become expensive. The extra paper can be a hassle since you have to carry it around, and you need enough copies for everyone. Lastly, I've been to many presentations where I was handed anywhere from one sheet of paper to an entire three ring binder full. With very few exceptions, all that paper ended up in the trash. While your presentation may be the best in the world, it's highly unlikely the audience will keep anything you've handed out. Something to consider.

Section 5

Kick Ass Way to Move and Talk

CHAPTER 22
What Comes Out of Your Mouth

The moment you step to the front of the class or onto the stage, all eyes are upon you. You haven't even uttered a word and yet the presentation has begun. You will have the full attention of everyone there. But in exchange for their continued attention, the audience will want something in return. What will it be? Information, humor, excitement, emotion, thought provoking content, an actionable how-to, or a recipe for a fabulous chocolate cake? Give the audience what they want and you'll be rewarded with their continued focus and attention. Lose control of the room, and your audience will punish you by looking at their watches, talking with each other, or checking email on their cell phones. In order to win over the audience, you will have to take control!

➤Command Presence

I was in my late thirties when I was taking a college class on modern technology (one of those easy "A" elective courses). Our class was divided into groups of three and we had to prepare a presentation on some topic of our choosing, presumably modern technology. I was paired up with two nice guys, both in their early twenties, who as far as I could tell, lacked any presentation experience. When it was time for our group to present, the first guy went up and did a good job conveying his portion of the presentation. It was nothing fancy, but at that point, our group was on par with the groups that had gone before us.

Unfortunately, the second guy in our group didn't fare as

well. He came prepared with a written speech and proceeded to do exactly what I beg you not to do. He read his speech aloud to the class. As was predictable, his first few lines were strong and were presented with enthusiasm. But as he rambled along, he became fatigued. He leaned his elbows on the table in front of himself and spoke to the class with his face pointed downward into his paper. Soon, he was practically lying on the table and his voice was barely audible. I was surprised the instructor didn't step in and administer some sort of CPR. By the time he finished reading his script, I feared that my presentation partner had killed my chance for an easy "A" on this assignment.

When my partner was finally done torturing the class, it was my turn to carry us to the finish line. I stepped to the front of the class. When I scanned the room, I saw that several of my classmates had their heads down on their desks, while others looked as if they had just seen a horrific car crash. One student held up her fingers in the shape of a gun, placed them to her head, and pulled the trigger. I knew that our team was in trouble and I needed to do something to pull us out of the hole.

I stood for a moment, took a deep breath, and with a deep and thunderous voice, I bellowed, "Hello, I'm Brian Stampfl, and for my portion of our presentation I will..." And off I went. Between the volume, tone, and the solid delivery of material, I not only regained the attention of the class, I even shocked my teacher back to life! I knew my material, all five minutes' worth, and was determined to deliver my message whether the class wanted to hear it or not. I spoke with passion and was determined to save the day. My classmates were going to learn something new and I was there to teach them. And for a solid five minutes, I had taken control of the room. I did so through Command Presence!

Knowledge of Material, Solid Delivery, Passion

So that I don't leave you with the impression that Command Presence is simply yelling at your classmates, let me clarify.

Command Presence is the pride that you'll feel knowing that your presentation is solid and that you know your material better than anyone else in the room. Fear of being asked a question you can't answer is gone, simply because you'll know the answer. And if for some reason you don't consider yourself an authority on the subject matter, you'll fake it. You will never let on that you're not the expert. You'll be in control and your audience will know it.

Command Presence is not a loud voice mowing over your audience. *It's an attitude.* And it's that attitude that gives you the power to speak loud enough to ensure everyone can hear you. It's the power to speak clearly so your message is heard. Your attitude is also your unspoken order to your audience to put down their smart phones, sit up straight, pay attention, and listen to what you have to say. It's the confidence you'll feel knowing that you can't and won't fail. Once again, you're in control here.

While my description of Command Presence may sound like I'm describing a drill instructor, I'm really not. What I'm describing is the culmination of your practice, your knowledge, your desire to do a great job, and your determination to deliver.

➤Know Your Stuff - But Don't Memorize Your Stuff

I realize that I've been harping on you about knowing

your topic and the importance of being able to present your material as if you were an authority. However, I must warn you about a common mistake made by those new to public speaking. While it's critical that you know your material extremely well to ensure your success, DO NOT memorize your presentation word for word.

Through your preparation and practice, you'll be speaking about a topic that you've come to know well. And while you will know ahead of time what you're going to be taking about, it should not be scripted. Instead, I recommend a delivery method we'll call *Free Form Speaking*.

Imagine that I've asked you to describe the car you drive or the home you live in. I suspect you should have no problem. When you speak to the audience, it should be the same way. For example, when you get to your bullet point that says, *Three Categories of Pacific Northwest Pines*, you should simply begin speaking about the categories in the same manner you would describe your car. Tell people about the pines trees, don't ramble off a memorized script.

Why Memorizing A Script Will Tank Your Presentation

Memorizing your presentation is the equivalent of turning your assignment into a school play. The exception being if you forget your lines, there'll be no one on the sidelines ready to feed them to you to get back on track. Secondly, anyone who memorizes their script tends to sound as if they have memorized a script. It's very easy to detect and a turn-off for listeners.

Unlike an actual script for a play or television show, presentations are non-fiction and don't contain characters. There is no built in emotion, inflection, or motivation that would otherwise drive the characters. Despite the speaker's best efforts, the result is a monotone delivery.

Lastly, I've noticed that those who memorize their material will often show signs of trying to recall the information. This usually presents itself in the form of the speaker looking up and to the left in an attempt to recall their next line. This will generally override any attempt to connect with your audience, and is only one step above showing up with a piece of paper and reading your presentation out loud.

CHAPTER 23
The Screen Is Not Your Audience

Your PowerPoint presentation is dialed in. Each slide is packed full of message but void of excessive text. Your images are crisp and the video is primed for viewing. This is your finest work on display for all to see. But there's a problem.

What you project onto the big screen is not only a guide for your audience to follow along with you, it's your guide to help you stay on track. With each slide advance, you'll likely want to look up at the screen to ensure that the slide actually did change. And you may find yourself eyeballing the screen as you come to each of your bullet points. Who can blame a speaker for wanting to peer at a video or beautiful image as it's being displayed in all its glory? But with all this peeking and looking over your shoulder, at what point will you look at the audience?

The problem is that while looking up at the screen, speakers will sometimes become mesmerized by their own images, or are simply too dependent on the notes they've created for themselves. The speaker becomes drawn to the screen and forgets to turn back around and address their audience. The audience then has to look at the presenter's back side for the duration of the program. I've been an audience member on a few occasions where this happened. The distraction of having the speaker's back to the audience became the focal point of the presentation. It may not seem like such a big mistake, but it's a large bummer for the audience.

Use what you've projected on the screen as a tool to keep

you on track with your presentation. Glancing up to the screen for a few moments, and even directing your audience's attention to specific details is completely acceptable. But don't forget where your audience is sitting and be sure to speak to them.

➤Never Read to Your Audience

I've also had the misfortune of sitting through numerous presentations in which the presenter pasted what appeared to be book passages into their PowerPoint slides. Like clockwork, the same presenter then decided that it was necessary to *read* the entire text to the audience, sending the majority of the audience into a coma. If you've not experienced this firsthand, consider yourself lucky. Here are some reasons why reading to your audience is a disastrous way to do business.

Your Audience Knows How to Read - If for some reason you absolutely must put large amounts of text on the screen, let the audience read it themselves. Direct their attention to what it is you want them to read, and then give them time to do so. Once they're done, you can begin talking about the topic. If you need to reference a portion of the text on the screen, read only a small portion and paraphrase the rest. Don't fall into the trap of reading out loud what you just asked your audience to read themselves.

Most People Stink at Reading Out Loud - Reading out loud is not easy. The tendency is for the speaker to start out strong and speak the first few sentences without much trouble. Then they get fatigued or become self-conscious. The speed begins to fluctuate, the volume of the voice goes down, and the misspoken words and stutters start to kick in. By the time the paragraph is complete, the speaker sounds as if they have a sock stuffed in their mouth.

Large Amounts of Text Screams Laziness - Any yahoo can cut and paste large amounts of information into a slide, or type out all the things they hope to say during their presentation. But to trim down your words to a few per slide takes work, and your audience will appreciate the effort.

Clarification Alert!
I want to make it clear there is a difference between reading *to* your audience and speaking a few words that appear on the screen. For example, imagine reading an entire paragraph describing *Quantum Physics* to your audience versus simply saying the words *Quantum Physics* as they appear on a single slide. Nobody is going to be bothered that you read two or three words from your slide. But read an entire paragraph, and the crowd may turn on you. The same goes with your bullet point lists. If the bullet points are short and not full of complete sentences, you may be able to get away with reading aloud each point as you come to it. Even then, paraphrasing the bulleted text can minimize the feeling that you're reading to your audience.

➤Ah, Um, and You Know

Sometimes nerves can get to you. And you're welcome to be as nervous as you want, but don't let the audience know that you're stressed. The best way I've found to not sound nervous when speaking, is to listen to yourself as you speak. This may seem strange, but think about it. How often do we make an effort to actually listen to how we sound and hear the words that are coming out when we talk?

Try this experiment during your next conversation. When

you're speaking, deliberately avoid filling those moments when you're not sure what you're going to say with sounds such as *ah* and *um*. Instead, replace those moments when you feel stuck, with silence. Don't say anything in that brief moment while you decide what you'll say next. This conscious practice of eliminating *ah* and *um* from your normal speech pattern will make it easier to do so when you're presenting.

Don't be concerned that by eliminating filler noises you'll end up with long moments of silence. The reality is that saying *ah* or *um* takes only a split second. Avoiding those sounds leaves such an insignificant moment of silence between words or sentences that your audience won't even notice. And keep in mind that *ah* and *um* aren't even words, they're sounds. Which is a better choice when pausing to think about your next sentence, a moment of thoughtful reflection or caveman noises?

When someone frequently fills their breaks in speech with filler sounds, the audience will notice and they'll either feel bad for the speaker or be annoyed by them. In either case, filler sounds make the speaker sound as if they are nervous or unprepared. Keep in mind also that actual words used repeatedly to fill in gaps of time, such as *you know* or *okay,* will give the appearance you're not confident in what you have to say.

Lastly, if you're curious about how you sound when you speak, consider video recording yourself as you practice. You'll be surprised at how much you can learn by hearing and seeing yourself perform. Doing this prior to your presentation will give you a chance to fine-tune yourself by eliminating any odd movements or speech patterns you may otherwise not have been aware of.

CHAPTER 24
Practice for Time

When you're presenting, you'll find your sense of timing can be easily thrown off. Often, you'll end way too soon or run too late. Be aware of the following pitfalls to ensure you have 15 minutes of material to fill a 15 minute presentation.

Speed Kills
Most people tend to speak faster than they realize when they're first learning the craft of public speaking. This is a common symptom of nervousness. If you find yourself going faster on stage than during your practice sessions, that means the PowerPoint slide you dedicated one minute of discussion to, may actually take only 45 or 30 seconds to cover. If you figure a 15 - 30 second increase in speed for each slide, you'll be one and a half to three minutes ahead of schedule after just six slides, and three to six minutes after just twelve slides. Six minutes ahead of schedule may not seem like much, but it is when you've discovered that you've finished 40% earlier than planned.

Efficiency of Words
What you plan to say to your audience and what you actually say may turn out to be two different things. While in your preparation phase obviously, you'll decide what to say about your topic. Your practice sentences will be long and full of information. But when you go live, your brain may start streamlining your message to the audience. You'll begin speaking in your natural voice, abandoning all the extra words you don't use in normal speech. The result is a natural sounding, but shorter than expected presentation.

One More Question
It's helpful to know if the time allotted for your presentation includes the time you'll need to answer questions. I've found that inquiries from the audience can be really fun for a couple of reasons. First, if one person is asking, chances are that many people may be interested. It may be some profound thought that someone had while listening to you, or it may be a chance to correct confusion your audience may have.

Second, I've discovered that some of my question and answer exchanges have been better than any presentation that I could've created. These are the special occasions in which the audience members are totally engaged and have a genuine interest in the topic I'm knowledgeable about. It's a great feeling, but it also consumes precious minutes.

Unless you are experienced with adjusting your presentation time on the fly, I'd recommend holding off on all questions until the end. That way you can complete your presentation uninterrupted within the allotted time. At that point, you can take a deep breath and open the floor to questions with the time remaining. The good news is if you have just two minutes of extra time, you can cut off the questions at the two-minute mark and blame it on the clock. If the reverse happens to be true and you have extra time, you can elicit questions from the crowd to fill that space. Either way, holding off on questions until your presentation is completed gives you the control to fill the remaining time by putting the audience to work.

CHAPTER 25
Humor

One of the best bits of advice I was ever given about using humor was this:

Humor comes with great risk!

And while I enjoy using humor in my presentations, I've confirmed with firsthand experience that the risk is high and the loss, nerve-racking.

I will not encourage or discourage you from using humor in your presentation. If you can pull off a funny presentation, then heck, I'd like to see it myself. However, keep in mind what the main purpose of your presentation is. You are there to pass on information, whether it be for a grade, for business, or some other professional need. The message is first, the comedy is a way to make the sharing of information more fun. And whether you choose to incorporate humor really depends on your topic, your purpose for presenting, and the audience you'll be speaking to. Choose wisely my friend.

Humor Either Works or it Doesn't
Funny people are funny. If you happen to be a funny person, it's probable that you'll be able to insert some humor into your presentation and make it work. However, I have some suggestions on how you can improve your odds of not bombing like a wannabe comedian on open mic night.

Know your audience
I used to do a presentation in which I compared the current

crime scene television shows, such as CSI, Criminal Minds, and NCIS, to the reality of the actual business. With a topic like that, I found all kinds of humorous Hollywood-style exaggerations that I could make fun of. I got lots of laughs from the audience and the result was a fun presentation that I loved doing. I was a presenter and an aspiring comedy genius at the same time.

Through word of mouth, I was asked to present to a group of about 40 for a morning breakfast at a yacht club. They'd heard my presentation was interesting and wanted to hear it. I arrived early and introduced myself to as many people as I could ahead of time. Everyone was pleasant and thanked me for joining them. I also received numerous invitations to visit the breakfast buffet, since they always ended up with too much food.

When it was time to start, I was introduced to the audience and off I went. Within the first minute, I fired off a humorous TV show versus reality comparison. I paused and waited for the room to break into laughter, but nothing happened. I didn't panic, I just figured that it was early and the crowd needed to warm up a bit. I continued on, delivering my funniest lines for the entire thirty minutes. During that time, I got a few awkward smiles, but nobody was laughing. My proven performance fell flat, and for the first time, all my jokes bombed.

At the conclusion of my presentation, I received a gratuitous round of applause, and several more invitations to eat more food. I decided that since I was going to be there a little longer, I would try to figure out why no one thought my presentation was funny. So I started asking questions.

The audience was made up of an older group of people (think grandmas and grandpas). After simply asking what television shows they enjoyed watching, I quickly found out that most of the people didn't watch the crime shows I was referencing. They had no idea what I was talking about! Although I was talking about CSI Las Vegas and how silly that show can be, most of these folks were already in bed when it was airing. There was no laughter because there was no context. This was a complete oversight on my part and an example you should keep in mind when integrating humor into your presentation.

Know your audience.

Stop the Bleeding

The best part about trying to be funny during your presentation is that you can always stop trying. Audiences are filled with all kinds of people, and not all of them want to be entertained. It might be too early in the morning, or they may not have had their coffee. You might even have an audience filled with duds. Who knows? If you knock out a few clever comments, use your funniest of voices, or tell your best joke and don't get a response, change course. Do not force more humor down the throats of people who don't want to be entertained. Go back to what it is that you showed up for in the first place, and that's to give a great presentation.

Another thing: if you do bomb a joke, never apologize for it and just keep going. Trying to repair a funny comment that didn't get a response is the equivalent of apologizing for misspeaking or any other error you may commit. If you keep moving along as if nothing happened, the crowd will move along with you. Keep going and leave the humor for another occasion.

CHAPTER 26
Body Talk

A section on what to do with your body? Seriously, who can't figure that out? While it may seem like your body movement on stage should be a no-brainer, it's a serious point of concern for many. And for good reason. Where you stand, what you do with your hands, and how you move are all part of how you communicate your message.

If you don't think your body is an important part of your performance, imagine your favorite movie actress in a climactic scene where she confronts the bad guy. How impressive would she be telling the bad guy that she hasn't decided which of his kneecaps she's going to shoot first, while twisting her hair with her finger, looking down at the ground, and cowering in the corner? Strong dialogue is great, but not if you look like an introvert while delivering it. Just like your favorite actress, who is also a performer, your body needs to deliver your message as well as your words. And the best way to counteract what your body may be saying outside your awareness, is to take control of what your body is doing.

►Why We Do What We Do - A Primal Response

If public speaking scares the hell out of us, then it's reasonable to say what we do unconsciously with our bodies is likely a *fight or flight* response. Granted, when most speakers become nervous, they don't start throwing rocks at the audience, or hold up their fists and threaten to kick everyone's ass. That would be a *fight* response and not a very appropriate one if you hope to get an "A" in your class.

On the other hand, if a speaker unexpectedly jumps from the stage and escapes through a fire exit, or simply doesn't show up for their speaking engagement, that's a *flight* response. These actions might have a negative impact on your grade as well. But if we know we're going to be nervous, isn't it possible that we can identify our unconscious responses and mitigate the damage our caveman brains would have us suffer?

Or more simply stated: Can we control our bodies?

➤The Distance to Here

If we're going to talk about our bodies, the best place to start is where we should put them. Where you stand in relation to your audience will reflect your level of comfort and confidence. I personally like to move in close to the audience, being mindful not to invade personal space, and remain visible to everyone.

Of course, closing the gap between the audience and ourselves is the opposite of what fear would have us do. The nervous person may find themselves creating distance from the audience as they search for some unidentified comfort zone. And while moving back from the audience may not completely kill your presentation, it can feel awkward for those hoping to make a connection with you. The distance you create may be subtle, but the audience will sense that something's not quite right.

Luckily for us, most speaking environments limit the speaker's ability to step too far away. Having a wall to your back or the edge of a stage creates boundaries that will keep you from straying too far. If you're obligated to use a podium or stand next to a computer to advance your PowerPoint presentation, then your position on stage will be predetermined. In that case, you won't have to think about it. Otherwise, prior to your presentation, take a look at the environment and ask yourself where you would expect a speaker to stand if you were sitting in the audience. Once you've identified that spot, stand there. Now take two steps forward and you've arrived.

➤Building Barriers

Placing an object between yourself and the audience is another primal response designed to protect us from a perceived threat. *Shielding* can be accomplished by standing behind the podium, a microphone stand, a table, or any object available to the speaker. Less obvious methods of *shielding* include the speaker putting their hands into their pockets, the fig leaf pose, or folding their arms across their chest. All of these methods insert some sort of barrier between the speaker and the audience, thereby reducing the speaker's feeling of vulnerability. Be aware, there's a difference between someone standing behind a microphone stand and someone who is trying to hide behind it. The difference is subtle, but be assured, your audience will know the difference.

So, what should you be doing with your body?

➤What Do I Do With My Hands?

Outside of job interviews and public speaking, I don't think there's any other time in which we become so concerned about what we should be doing with our hands. For those not comfortable with public speaking, the hands can become a distraction for both you and your audience. Having both hands pressed into your pants pockets, fidgeting with a pen, or playing with your hair could convey to your audience that you're either unprepared or nervous. Below are a few steps you can take to avoid that look.

For the Men: Gentlemen, unfortunately we tend to violate most of the rules of hand etiquette while standing in front of groups of people. While the list of violations is long, I have a few all-encompassing recommendations that should help:

- Avoid standing with your hands folded over one another in front of your crotch. The *fig leaf* look is generally reserved for wedding photos.

- Avoid contact with your body that could be described by using the words *picking* or *digging*.

- Refrain from any attempt to adjust your underwear. Sticking your hands into your front pockets to surreptitiously make an adjustment will be detected by those in the front row.

- Most importantly, keep your hands away from your nose.

For the Women: Ladies, I'm happy to report that most of you do not suffer from the same bad habits often displayed by men. However, when nervous, women tend to overuse their hands and body to communicate. While the movements are generally natural, the line between conveying thought and an aerobic workout is not always clear. Just be sure to relax and make sure your hand gestures don't appear excessive.

And don't mess with your hair!

So What Should You Do With Your Hands?

Let them move freely as you speak. Hand gesturing is a completely natural part of communication. The gestures will allow you to place emphasis on the points you're trying to make, relay emotions, and even create imagery for your audience. Most of the communication that comes through your body is done unconsciously. Forcing your hands to remain at your sides or some other place will feel and look unnatural. Once you allow yourself the freedom of movement, while avoiding the previously listed pitfalls, you'll find that your audience will see you as being comfortable, and you'll feel more relaxed yourself.

➤Focus on Your Eyes

If I hadn't actually met aspiring presenters who've spent an inordinate amount of time thinking about this small detail, it would never have occurred to me to address it. And to my surprise, I've actually been asked the question, "What should I do with my eyes?"

I guess it's a fair question, especially after covering the equally complex question of, *What Do I Do With My Hands?* Our eyes say so much about us, and it makes sense that we'd like to have some control over what message they're relaying to the audience. Rather than allowing our beady little eyes to dart around uncontrollably like caffeine-infused squirrels, we need to have a plan for our untrained eyeballs.

The most common concern regarding the eyes is simply wanting to know where to look when speaking to a crowd. There are several answers, and therefore several approaches, to eyeball management.

Scan Wide, Scan Deep
Audiences want to see you, and on the flip side, they want to

be seen. It's all part of that connection thing I promise you is the difference between a good and exceptional presentation.

The first thing I recommend is that you force yourself to see the full width and depth of the crowd. That is, make sure you focus your attention not only on those in the middle of the audience, but those off to the left, right, front, and to the back. It's too easy to simply look straight ahead, never acknowledging or making eye contact with those not seated dead center.

To ensure that you get full coverage, visualize the entire seating area divided into sections. Depending on the size of the audience, this may be as simple as dividing the room in half, with audience members to your left and right. With larger crowds, you may find yourself with three sections (right, middle, left) or six sections representing front left, back left, middle front, back front, etc. Focus your attention on one section at a time, then move on to the next. With practice, you'll find yourself doing this without much thought.

What Should I See?
As you're scanning the crowd, pick out people who are looking directly at you. Make eye contact with them, hold it for a few moments, and then move on to the next person. Once that momentary contact is made, you will know instinctively the impact you are having on that person. Are they interested, disinterested, sleepy, confrontational, confused, or wanting to walk out? You'll know because you'll be employing a skill you already have, and that's the ability to quickly size up people. Trust me, we are constantly making assessments of others, both strangers and those we know. As you make your assessment, you'll be drawn back to the ones who are supportive and interested. You'll actively seek out those same people so you can continue to receive the love, or at least support, those people have to offer. It's a great feeling

and the best part of public speaking.

But I Can't Look 'Em In The Eye
If you're not ready to make direct eye contact with your audience, try looking at each person's nose instead. It's a subtle difference, but should help if you're finding that direct eye contact is distracting. And don't worry about getting caught staring at people's noses. At any distance beyond six feet, it's impossible for someone to tell whether you're looking into their eyes or at their nose.

➤Control Your Body

Your body, like your hands, has to move.

When I present, I find it quite natural to move and walk around. Not only do I use my hands when I speak, I use my body in the same way to convey my message. I make it a point to walk around so I can be sure to make eye contact with each of my audience members, working to create that desired connection I've been talking about. But as I'm moving, I'm careful not to block anyone's view of the screen. If this is unavoidable, then I'll do so for only a short time and move on. I also avoid parking myself in any of the extreme corners of the room or stage.

Keep in mind that when I say I'm moving around, it's not a forced movement. It's about being comfortable and free to move as I choose. I personally tend to move towards people as I make eye contact with them. By doing so, I'm letting them know, *Yes, I see you and we have a connection.* I find it so much easier to deliver my message by walking around rather than being stuck in one location.

Be careful however, that walking around doesn't

transition into pacing. I know this can happen since I've caught myself doing it. Move freely, but don't travel between two fixed points on the stage.

Earlier in the *Studying the Greats - Develop Your Style* section, I referenced Robin William's performance. I hope you took the time to watch the video, and if not, it's well worth checking out. Imagine if he were to give that same performance but was forced to stand in one place. Although the words he speaks are fabulous, his genius comes through his body, thereby turning his presentation into a performance. Allowing yourself that same freedom of movement will make you a better speaker. I highly recommend it.

But What if There's No Place to Go?
Sometimes the environment dictates how much or how little you're able to move around. Depending on the occasion, you might be obligated by your instructor to stand at a podium, or there may not be much room for you to walk around. If you find yourself locked down, but have the ability to make changes to fit your needs, do it. It costs nothing to move a table, a chair, or make some other adjustment to your environment when possible. That additional freedom of movement will not only benefit you, it'll likely benefit your audience as you provide a better product.

A Word of Warning!
DO NOT position yourself so that your audience is forced to twist in their chairs in order to see you. And NEVER stand behind your audience while speaking.

I sat through a training seminar in which the presenter stood directly behind us the entire time. The result was a constant struggle by the audience to turn around in an attempt to locate the speaker. It's a creepy feeling to have a speaker stand behind you. Doing so will make your audience feel uncomfortable, and there's no way you're going to make a connection with them if they can't see you.

CHAPTER 27
What Not to Wear

Ten years ago, I would've told you that what a presenter wore during their speech made no difference whatsoever. If you'd asked, I would've said, "They're giving a frickin' speech! Who gives a rip what they're wearing?" Times have changed. More specifically, I got old and then started teaching.

Old People and Teachers Want You to Dress Nice

While you may be a brilliant speaker, appearing to care about how you look may in fact score you some extra points. I can tell you firsthand that when any of my students took the extra time to dress nicely for their presentations, I noticed. And yes, the extra effort can have a positive effect on the student's grade. Why? Because presenting is half visual and half audible. You're presenting an entire package. Even if you're not being graded, I can assure you that you'll be sized up by your appearance.

If you think I'm making this stuff up and need a second opinion, here's one. My accounting teacher announced to our class that business attire should be worn during our class presentations. He said that in the business world, no accountant would stand before a board of directors, telling them about the millions of dollars they made that year, wearing shorts and a T-shirt. We all understood the boardroom analogy, and since our teacher was willing to deduct points from our group's grade for not dressing appropriately, we opted to look sharp.

Look Like You Know What You're Talking About

As someone who generally dresses like a slob on most days, it's ironic to think that I might be offering up fashion advice. However, I should define what it means to dress nicely. Feel free to break away from my generic descriptions below, but be warned; if your teacher is over the age of 40, a concert T-shirt will not be considered dress attire, even if it's clean.

Business Attire - That is my recommendation for most situations, including the classroom. However, if you're presenting in any sort of a professional environment, including business seminars or training, or even defending your thesis project, business attire is a must. There are two types of business dress, *Business Casual* and *Business Professional*. Business Casual will work for most classroom situations. Business Professional is for those who really want to step up their game.

For the Men
Business Casual - slacks, long sleeve shirt, tie, dress shoes and belt
Business Professional - suit, dress shoes and belt

For the Women
Business Casual - slacks, blouse, closed-toe dress shoes
Business Professional - Pants or dress suit, blouse, closed-toe dress shoes

Both Men and Women - keep jewelry to a minimum. This includes large collections of ear and facial piercings, or any other adornments that may draw attention away from your presentation. Hair should be clean and neat.

If you've been rolling your eyes at my recommendations and think that business attire is overkill, then how about this?

Simply dress nicer than you would on any other day. If your instructor see's that you've made the effort to do something others in your class did not, it just might help get you a few extra points or a higher grade.

Exception Alert!
But what about costumes? While I've not had the opportunity to dress up in an outfit or wear some item representative of my speaking topic, I know of people who have. It's an unusual approach, but if done right it can make your performance much more interesting.

For example, dressing up as a historical figure or wearing clothing consistent with a certain time period could be a great way to enhance your performance. You may have clothing available that ties into your topic or is representative of a specific profession, sport, fictitious character, activity, or culture. Just be careful your costume efforts don't come across as silly, unless of course that's the look you're going for.

Before you make the decision to dress up for your presentation, please be thoughtful of your audience and who might be affected by your choice. Showing up to class dressed as a Nazi soldier or wearing clothing from a culture not your own may be offensive to some. There's no need to stress out your audience before you've even started speaking, and doing so is not going to earn you extra points.

Keep in mind that in order for your costume or topic-specific clothing to work, it's not enough to just show up wearing your outfit. If you step onto the stage dressed as a cowboy, a nurse, a US President, or a nineteenth century shopkeeper, you're going to have to introduce your outfit to the audience in some manner. For example, if you're dressed as a cowboy, you wouldn't simply state, "I'm a cowboy."

There has to be a connection between your outfit and your presentation. What you might say is, "This is the type of clothing that ranchers wore during the late eighteen hundreds." On the other hand, if you've dressed up as Abraham Lincoln and there's no mistaking who you are, explaining what you're wearing or even introducing your character won't be necessary.

If you have an authentic article of clothing that has more importance than just its appearance, you'll want to let your audience know that. For example, "This is an actual coal miner's helmet from the 1940s." In order to take full advantage of any special clothing items you choose to wear, it's important to understand they're not just clothing items. They're props and need to be showcased as such. Be sure to read the chapter on *Props* if you want to learn more about how to work props into your presentation.

Section 6

Kick Ass Art of
Audience Engagement

CHAPTER 28
The Art of Audience Engagement

One of the biggest gifts your audience can give you is to actively participate in your presentation. That is, ask you questions as you go along or answer the engagement-type questions you pose to them, such as, "How many of you have ever played the lottery?"

It's an incredible feeling knowing that your audience has an interest in what you have to say, or is willing to take themselves out of their own comfort zone to answer out loud the questions you pose to them. It's this relationship forged with the audience that inspires me to use the terms *presentation* and *performance* interchangeably. It's also that relationship that has allowed me to go from being a nervous beginner to someone who actually gets a rush out of presenting.

However, not all audiences are ready to give as much to you as you give to them. Sometimes you first need to establish a connection in order to have that relationship.

➤The Three Types of Crowds

When it comes to audience participation, you're going to experience one of three types of crowds. There's *The Hot Crowd*, *The Warm Crowd*, and *The Cold Corpse Crowd*.

Regardless of who you happen to draw, if audience participation is a critical part of your presentation and success, then you're going to need to know how to get these folks to come out and play!

1. The Hot Crowd - These are the fun ones and require little or no work on your part to get them to participate. These folks will laugh at your jokes, answer any question you ask, and generally have a great time. It's a fun environment to be in and really relieves the pressure if you're nervous about presenting. Just keep in mind if you're being graded (or being paid to speak), you may have to prevent the rowdy ones from hijacking your presentation and turning it into a party. I've had a couple of presentations go completely off track due to rowdy crowds. But since much of what I speak about falls under the heading of "infotainment," I don't mind loosening up a little bit and going off script. As long as the discussion comes back to the topic I started on, I'm okay with this.

2. The Warm Crowd - This is the most common group that you'll come across. These are usually just good folks who are interested in hearing what you have to say, but didn't necessarily plan on being part of the presentation. With *The Warm Crowd*, I've found that about one-fourth of the audience, regardless of size, is interested in participating. However, you'll need to establish a rapport with these people before you can have running dialogue with them.

Keep in mind that audience members often have their own fear of public speaking. Singling out someone, even willing participants, can cause them to become uncomfortable. Get the audience to warm up to you first, then identify those who are willing to interact with you.

I've found the best way to get the audience to engage in conversation is to ask broad-based questions that will likely have a large number of positive responses. For example:

"Who here has one or more pets at home?"

This is a simple, non-threatening question, likely to yield a high number of hands being raised. Of course, I recommend asking questions that pertain to your topic. The pet question may not be appropriate if your topic is *Microwave Cooking Techniques*. In that case, you could ask a question like:

"Who here would like to learn how to cook a family meal in under twenty minutes?"

In a perfect world, everyone in the audience would raise their hands after the question has been posed. But in this case, we're looking for those who'd most likely be willing to engage with you, whether it's to answer your questions, ask their own questions, or have a topic-related discussion as part of your presentation. Those that raise their hands are the ones most likely to talk to you. Treat these people well. When you finally decide to engage an individual, such as asking them their opinion about a topic, those that are excited to interact with you will do so brilliantly. But if you pick someone and sense that they're uncomfortable speaking in front of everyone, give them an out and move on to someone else. It's all about building a good relationship with your audience.

3. The Cold Corpse Crowd - I hope that you don't run into this group, and odds are you won't. This is the type of audience that often exists when attendance is mandated and the topics are of little interest to them. Think work conferences, re-certifications, and job training as an example. On the other hand, sometimes the audience is just filled with duds. They don't care that you're hosting a party...they're party poopers.

The good news is there are ways to handle audiences who are generally disinterested. Of course, if you have no intention of interacting with your audience or taking questions, *The Cold Corpse Crowd* might work out well for you. You talk and they can sit quietly and pout. But as I see it, it's our job as presenters to get people to change their state of mind and loosen up. You have something to offer and the audience darn well needs to receive it. But that's not to say it's easy to accomplish.

While voluntary participation of your audience may be part of your plan, realize that it's not a requirement for success. You'll want to employ all the tricks you've learned for getting your audience to open up and have an exchange of dialogue with you.

The first step in cracking *The Cold Corpse Crowd* is the same as with *The Warm Crowd*. Start off with broad-based questions. Even if the question is as benign as, "Who here has one or more pets at home?", be prepared that you may not get any responses. When this happens, simply be patient, stand quietly and wait for a response. Scan the room and make eye contact with as many people as you can and wait. The waiting will serve three purposes.

First, it will serve as a message to your audience that you will be posing questions to them and that you'll be standing by for answers. By pausing, you're also giving your audience permission to either raise their hand or respond with an answer. As I've said before, audience members can suffer from stage fright as well, and may be hesitant to say anything in front of other people for fear they'll be wrong or otherwise embarrassed.

Secondly, your pause will create an awkward tension in the room. This comes when people realize that you've asked a question and their lack of response is holding you up. Someone may say something just to break the tension.

Lastly, the pause will allow you to take advantage of the human brain's inability to not answer questions. This may seem strange, but it's true. The human brain cannot leave a question unanswered. Think about watching a game show on television with family or friends. When the question is asked, what do most people do if they know the answer? They blurt it out! Even when everyone agrees not to yell out the answer, what do they do instead? They wiggle around on the couch, and proclaim, "I know this one! I know this one!"

I'm not a psychologist, but the way I see it, even though no one from the audience has spoken up to answer your question, be assured that everyone has formulated an answer in their mind. Your job is to give the audience permission to say what they're thinking. Waiting for their answer *is* that permission.

Once you get the first person to interact with you, others will feel at ease and hopefully join in. I can't guarantee that you'll have full audience participation, but a few people are all you need to keep your presentation moving.

Help, I can't crack the nut!

It's entirely possible that you'll run into a crowd that flat out refuses to participate. While the pause technique generally works well, you can't stand there in silence forever. At some point you'll have to get back to speaking. If you find yourself in this position, accept that you've got yourself a tough crowd. But once again, there are solutions.

If the audience refuses to interact with you, you'll simply need to interact with...yourself.

If you pose a question such as, "What type of music did you listen to in high school?" and you don't get an answer even after your pause, answer the question yourself. This is your transition from the pause, back to your presentation. Your response could be something along the lines of, "Although I like a variety of music, I mostly listened to rock."

By answering your own question, you'll have received your needed answer and will have kept the conversation going. When the time comes, pose your next question to the crowd and use your pause technique again. If you don't get a response, answer the question yourself again and continue on with your presentation.

While this may sound like an insane way of delivering a presentation, it's a surprisingly smooth way of transitioning out of the problem caused by lack of audience participation. Done correctly, the conversation you'll essentially be having with yourself can, in fact, sound natural to your audience. However, you'll have to decide how many times you're willing to do this before you gain audience participation. If you reach your limit, don't be discouraged. Focus on being an amazing presenter and forge ahead to the end.

➤Taming a Wild Audience

If your plan is to simply give your presentation and take a few questions at the end, I hope the audience is polite and supportive of your effort to do your best. But whether it's in the classroom or a packed auditorium, there's always a chance you'll encounter that one person who is dying to participate, whether you want them to or not. Most of the people who will raise their hands during your presentation are awesome and are there to support you. Others are awkwardly inquisitive, some can't sit quietly for ten minutes, a few are obnoxious, and once in a while, the audience simply takes on a life of its own.

Knowing what this behavior looks like and having a response already planned will give you the power to keep your presentation on track. Here are some of the more common personalities and audience tendencies that you may encounter, with a few suggestions on how to address them.

The Green Gorilla Guy - This is the person that asks impossible hypothetical questions about your topic. While they probably won't ask about a Green Gorilla per se, this term describes the absurdity of the question itself. These types of questions are easy to notice since both you and your audience will initially feel compelled to roll your eyes in reaction. As an example, if the topic is *The Benefits of Mass Transit,* the question might sound something like this:

"What if a Green Gorilla jumps into the front seat while the driver is in the bathroom and steals the bus?"

Resolution - I don't recommend any attempt to embarrass any of your audience members. While it might be tempting, you should refrain from snarky responses or insults. Keep in mind that although the question might sound goofy to you, the person may be sincere in asking. I often have to remind myself that, *Not all things obvious to me are obvious to others.* For that reason, sensitivity is key.

I've found that addressing the question as if it were legitimate, while pointing out why the scenario is unlikely, works fairly well. By doing so, you've answered the question asked, while pointing out the glaring unlikeliness of it. These are some possible responses to the Green Gorilla bus theft question:

"While having the bus stolen would be highly inconvenient, it's also very unlikely since drivers are prohibited from making personal stops prior to their final destination."

OR

"It would be difficult for someone to steal the bus, at least quickly, since it takes several minutes for the air brake system to obtain full pressure. Hopefully, the driver would have returned by then."

The Private Conversation Guy - This person will raise their hand not to ask questions about your topic, but rather to ask questions that are of personal interest to themselves only. For example, you might be a photographer having just returned from Australia and your presentation is on endangered species. Rather than inquire about your research into the endangered Speckled Dingo, he'll ask where he can buy used photography gear at a good price.

<u>Resolution</u> - This one is easy since the person appears to have some interest in your expertise. Simply give a quick, short answer to their question and then invite them to speak with you at the end of the presentation. It might sound something like this:

"I have a few ideas where you might acquire inexpensive equipment. I have a few questions of you, though. Let's talk at the end of the presentation."

I Have a Question, and a Better Answer Guy - This is a scenario that's best described through a real life example. I was attending a forensic science conference in Minneapolis. One of the courses was on firearms identification. Rest assured that the presenter's resume was exceptional and that he was well qualified to teach the class. He was what you might call...an expert.

As the presentation was moving along, a gentleman in the crowd raised his hand to ask a question. When he was called on, the gentleman asked the presenter if he knew about some custom modification to a firearm no one had ever heard of. The presenter paused for a moment and simply acknowledged that he was not familiar with what the gentleman had described.

Unfortunately, the gentleman saw this as a "gotcha" moment for the presenter, and took the opportunity to stand up and lecture the audience for a full minute with his inconsequential drivel. This guy had literally asked a question he knew the presenter would not have known about, just to show the presenter and the audience how smart he was!

Resolution - Some people are just dying for attention. In this case, the gentleman likely thought of himself as an expert and wanted to establish himself as such. The best approach to this problem is to publicly acknowledge the gentleman's brilliance (whether justified or not) and redirect the presentation back to yourself. It might sound like this:

"You're certainly very knowledgeable about this subject. However, I think that we've gotten more technical than what I'd hoped to cover in this presentation. We'll continue on."

OR

"That's very interesting. You obviously know a lot about this subject. However, since the audience may not have that level of expertise, I'll continue with a more basic approach."

It works well to stroke the offender's ego by telling the audience exactly what he wanted them to know. He's an expert too. As recommended, embarrassing a member of the audience is not advised. Telling this guy he's out of line or that he's not as brilliant as he believes is not going to benefit anyone. The goal is to gain back control and not get into an argument. Lastly, by telling the offender that you'll be returning back to the basics of the topic, it's one more way of saying, "I know you're amazing, but we'll need to focus on the simple stuff for the rest of the audience."

The Rowdy Crowd Takeover - Once in a while you'll come across a group that gets caught up in their own self-generated entertainment. That is, someone in the crowd will make a comment, and then someone else decides to one-up that guy with their own witty remark. These two start chirping back and forth, usually all in good fun, and others from the crowd jump in with their two cents. Luckily, this silliness usually lasts for less than a minute.

<u>Resolution</u> - Have fun with it. Each time I've experienced this, I found the people in the audience were quite funny and were having a great time. Following a few inquiries, I often learned the audience was made up of co-workers or good friends. As long as the crowd is laughing and having fun, they're going to attribute the fun to you, anyway. Let it play out until the laughter settles down. Then break back in and continue on with the presentation. If you experience repeat offenses to the point of disruption, just let the audience know you have a limited amount of time and need to continue on.

The Non-Stop Question Guy - I think we've all taken a class with this guy. Need I say more?

<u>Resolution</u> - This one may be the easiest to deal with. You may find yourself taking several questions from this guy before you realize his plan is to pepper you with questions ad nauseam. But once you see the pattern, you can politely say:

"I'm very interested in answering your questions. However,

I'll take questions if we have time at the end of the presentation."

OR

"I have a section coming up addressing that exact question. If you wait until then, we'll get it covered."

OR

"I appreciate your questions. However, I have limited time to cover all my material and need to keep moving."

The Confronter - This person takes advantage of having the attention of a large group of people to address their personal needs or complaints. I witnessed this personally while attending a fundraising event. Following a speech by the president of the organization, the floor was opened to the audience for questions about the organization and the benefits of the money being raised. One audience member went into a five minute diatribe about how the organization was not servicing her specific interests. To top it off, this woman starting crying and created an uncomfortable situation for everyone.

Resolution - Kudos to the president of the organization who handled the situation perfectly, and I recommend this approach, as well. First, she acknowledged this woman's concerns as being legitimate. It didn't matter whether the president thought the woman was right or not, but rather that her concerns were real. To do otherwise would likely have embarrassed the woman and turned the situation into an argument.

The president went on to explain to everyone in the audience the charity's mission within the community they served, but said that she was open to discussing ways to expand the charity's distribution of benefits. Keep in mind the president did not make a promise of immediate change, but rather, was open to discussing it.

Lastly, the president asked to speak with the woman privately following the event. This may be the most important part of the resolution. Why? Remember, our goal here is to take back control of the presentation. This is a polite and professional way of letting everyone know that the conversation between the president and the woman will continue, just not at that moment.

While this specific example occurred at a fundraiser in which a presentation was being given, this approach is a good one anytime someone wants to challenge you or discuss things that have nothing to do with your topic.

Low Probability
With all the different ways that an audience can disrupt your presentation, it may seem as if there's a high probability that you're going to run into problems. The reality is that your chance of having someone give you a bad time is very low. While I've either personally experienced or witnessed all of the behaviors I've listed above, they were generally isolated to large-scale events.

If your presentation is for a class or some other small, non-business event, you're most likely going to be in the company of good people. They will likely be interested in your topic, will want you to succeed, and will ask thoughtful questions. And except for *The Non-Stop Question Guy*, you should have nothing to worry about. But then again, be prepared just in case.

CHAPTER 29
Crash and Burn - When Things Go Wrong

If you follow the guidelines in this book, I'm confident that you'll deliver a rock star performance. Your audience will love you, your teacher will shower you with straight A's, and you'll have reached legendary status among your peers. You'll be regarded as a model of speaking perfection. But then again, things don't always work out as planned.

The good news is that there are very few things that can go wrong that can't be corrected on the fly. Sometimes the problem will be of your own doing and sometimes not. Part of being an amazing presenter is the ability to mitigate unexpected problems as they arise. While throwing up your hands, crying, dropping the F-Bomb, or walking off the stage mid-performance may be options for some when things don't go their way, finding ways to work through problems will be your secret to success. Even the world's greatest skydivers carry a back-up parachute and I suggest you have a back-up plan as well. Knowing the solutions ahead of time to the most common problems will give you the confidence to know you cannot fail.

➤What the Crowd Don't Know, the Crowd Don't Know

In the event something does go wrong during your presentation, don't air your dirty laundry! Unless the building is on fire (something you should probably mention), don't draw attention to mistakes you've made or technical problems you're experiencing. I've seen firsthand where the presenter encountered some insignificant problem and obsessed over it rather than just fixing it and moving on. The likelihood is most of your audience will not even be aware of the problem you're experiencing.

And for all your minor mishaps (and they're all minor mishaps), I offer a simple two-part solution to keep you moving forward.

Fix or dismiss the problem. Move on.

That's it. If you stumble over your microphone cord, dismiss it and move on. If the batteries in your projector remote die, use the computer's space bar to advance your slides. If you forget to mention a key point early on, mention it when you can or forget about it. Whatever you do if a problem arises, fix it or forget it and move on. The less time you spend fussing with a problem, the less likely anyone will know it exists. But if someone does notice the minor mishap, don't worry, the audience is not going to care. They want you to succeed.

I'll say that again.

The audience doesn't care if you make a mistake.

Every person in the audience has a life. They make mistakes, you make mistakes, we all do. How you work through minor mishaps will determine if you're a beginner or on your way to turning pro.

►When You've Forgotten Everything You Know

"What was I talking about?" You may think it, but don't pose that question to your audience.

Losing your place while speaking or forgetting what you were going to say is a real possibility. It happens to the best of us. But the recovery is doable. First off, don't ask the audience for guidance. Just pause for a moment and see if you remember where you left off. Keep in mind that while you're pausing to regroup, time will be a bit skewed. You may feel that any amount of time you spend sitting idle will seem like minutes when in fact it's only a few seconds. Time distortion is a symptom of stress. Don't let it turn to panic.

If a momentary pause and scan of your memory doesn't bring you to where you left off, remember your PowerPoint presentation comes with built-in safety nets. The pictures and text act as your outline, guiding you along as you speak. Allow that information to bring you back where you left off. Once you figure out what you should be saying, start back up and keep on going. Don't apologize for the pause and don't do anything to draw attention to the error.

➤Tongue-Tied

Getting tongue-tied or misspeaking is likely the most common mistake you're going to make. However, misstating a statistic or mispronouncing a word is so easily correctable, it can hardly be called a mistake. Once you realize your error, simply correct yourself without skipping a beat.

"Excuse me. What I meant to say is that *most* mammals live between..."

"Correction. 45% of people living in the..."

"What I meant to say is that of the top five fastest cars..."

What you'll find is that this type of error and correction are consistent with normal conversation. Because this solution is so fluid, most people won't even recognize or remember that the error occurred. But if you throw up your hands or demonstrate your frustration, that's the equivalent of waving a red flag and creating a memory for your audience to take home with them. If you find you're experiencing multiple occasions in which the words don't come out right, it may be that you're speaking too fast. Slow down, make the corrections, and keep on going.

➤Proof That Recovery is Possible

I once presented at a conference to a group of about 35 people. As I was speaking, I felt as if I hadn't been able to establish a connection with the audience. I was getting little to or reaction to what I believed was fascinating information. This lack of response triggered a fear that my material was either not interesting or too basic for the audience. I thought I was boring my audience to death.

Because that wasn't stressful enough, I then realized I'd been moving along much faster than I had anticipated. I'd been asked to fill a 90 minute block of time, but at the rate I was going, I was likely to come in under 50 minutes. I was stressed!

Luckily for me, there was short break scheduled in the middle of my presentation. I approached two friends of mine in attendance, to plead with them to tell me what I was doing wrong. Now, it's important to know that these were good friends of mine, both of whom had speaking experience themselves. They're also the type of friends who'd not only be delighted to point out I was dying on stage, they'd laugh about it. That was the kind of honest feedback I needed at that moment. Not the gratuitous, "No, those pants don't make you look fat," kind of feedback you get when someone doesn't want to hurt your feelings.

To my surprise, when I told my friends how I was feeling, they just looked at me like I was wasting their time. Apparently they didn't see an opportunity to crush my soul, and simply told me I was doing fine and to quit whining. When I told them about my fear of not being able to fill my time, they suggested that I slow down and expand the details in my stories. Geniuses! It's good to have smart people in your life.

After the break, I walked back to the front of the room, took a deep breath, and continued my presentation. Per my friends' advice, I started by slowing down the rate I had been speaking. Then I lengthened my stories by simply adding details I originally thought I wouldn't have time for. It worked! Not only did I fill the time slot, the event coordinator had to tell me to wrap it up so I wouldn't run too long. At that point, half of my fears had been resolved.

After the presentation, I had several people come up to me to ask me questions and offer compliments. What I learned during our conversations was that much of the information I shared was new material for my audience, and that they were impressed by my experience and insight. I then realized I had misread the audience by thinking what I was saying was boring or too basic. As it turned out, the opposite was true.

It was proof that most problems are easily corrected, and most fears are unfounded.

Section 7

Kick Ass Show Time

CHAPTER 30
Showtime

You've done everything you can. Your topic has been decided and your outline is complete. The PowerPoint has been fine-tuned to perfection and transferred to your thumb drive. You have all the tools you need to not only deliver a high quality presentation, you have safety nets built in to assist you in the event you get stuck along the way. You've mastered the art of interacting with the audience and are ready to use their enthusiasm and energy to your advantage. This is not just a presentation, this is a performance. You are going to knock it out of the park.

Enjoy the experience. It's going to be awesome!

And when you're done, I want to hear about it. Seriously, send me an email and let me know how it went. I want to know what worked best for you, what new things you may have learned, and suggestions you may have developed for making your presentation great. I'd love to not only receive your feedback, I'd like to share it with others who may benefit from your real-life experience.

brian@kickasscollegeguide.com

Thank you for the opportunity to share my insights on presentations. I wish you the best of success. Now go Kick Ass!

➤Last Minute Checklist

As You're Running Out the Door

- Papers, Reports, Projects - to be turned in to your instructor.
- Handouts, Props, Show and Tell Items
- Presentation Notes, Note Cards
- Thumb Drives or Other Media With Your PowerPoint Presentation
- Laptop, Speakers, Projector, Required Cords
- Proper Attire and Appearance

When It's Your Turn to Speak

- Turn in Required Papers, Reports, Projects (as directed by instructor)
- Handouts to the Audience Before You Speak
- Load Your PowerPoint
- Stage Props and Show and Tell Items
- Turn Off Lights
- Stand Tall and Breathe
- Make a Connection With the Audience
- Kick Ass!

About the Author

Brian Stampfl is a law enforcement professional with a passion for presentations and public speaking. In addition to years of instructing, presenting and public speaking experience, he's a former adjunct faculty member at Seattle University, where he taught a course on Crime Scene Investigation.

Following numerous requests from students to help them prepare for their classroom presentations, Brian realized that there were few resources available to help students overcome the fear of public speaking and to create great presentations. This book, *The Kick Ass College Guide to Presentations*, is the solution to that problem.

Brian welcomes your comments and questions, and can be reached at brian@kickasscollegeguide.com

For additional presentation tips and tricks, updates on future projects and other fun stuff, join the Kick Ass College Guide email list at www.kickasscollegeguide.com

Made in the USA
San Bernardino, CA
25 July 2017